Kabbalistic Astrology

The Ultimate Guide to Hebrew Astrology for Beginners, Ancient Jewish Mysticism, Zodiac Signs, Interpreting Your Kabbalah Natal Chart, and Qabalistic Tarot Reading

© Copyright 2023 - All rights reserved.

The content contained within this book may not be reproduced, duplicated, or transmitted without direct written permission from the author or the publisher.

Under no circumstances will any blame or legal responsibility be held against the publisher, or author, for any damages, reparation, or monetary loss due to the information contained within this book, either directly or indirectly.

Legal Notice:

This book is copyright protected. It is only for personal use. You cannot amend, distribute, sell, use, quote or paraphrase any part, or the content within this book, without the consent of the author or publisher.

Disclaimer Notice:

Please note the information contained within this document is for educational and entertainment purposes only. All effort has been executed to present accurate, up-to-date, reliable, and complete information. No warranties of any kind are declared or implied. Readers acknowledge that the author is not engaging in the rendering of legal, financial, medical, or professional advice. The content within this book has been derived from various sources. Please consult a licensed professional before attempting any techniques outlined in this book.

By reading this document, the reader agrees that under no circumstances is the author responsible for any losses, direct or indirect, that are incurred as a result of the use of the information contained within this document, including, but not limited to, errors, omissions, or inaccuracies.

Your Free Gift
(only available for a limited time)

Thanks for getting this book! If you want to learn more about various spirituality topics, then join Mari Silva's community and get a free guided meditation MP3 for awakening your third eye. This guided meditation mp3 is designed to open and strengthen ones third eye so you can experience a higher state of consciousness. Simply visit the link below the image to get started.

https://spiritualityspot.com/meditation

Table of Contents

INTRODUCTION 1
CHAPTER 1: WHEN KABBALAH MEETS ASTROLOGY 3
CHAPTER 2: THE KABBALISTIC TREE OF LIFE..............................17
CHAPTER 3: SPHERES, PLANETS, AND STARS 35
CHAPTER 4: THROUGH THE ZODIAC I. CARDINAL SIGNS 42
CHAPTER 5: THROUGH THE ZODIAC II. FIXED SIGNS............................51
CHAPTER 6: THROUGH THE ZODIAC III. MUTABLE SIGNS....................56
CHAPTER 7: LESSONS OF THE LUNAR NODES 61
CHAPTER 8: READING THE KABBALISTIC NATAL CHART 69
CHAPTER 9: KABBALAH AND THE TAROT CARDS............................77
CHAPTER 10: QABALISTIC TAROT READING.................................96
CONCLUSION 107
HERE'S ANOTHER BOOK BY MARI SILVA THAT YOU MIGHT LIKE....109
YOUR FREE GIFT (ONLY AVAILABLE FOR A LIMITED TIME) 110
REFERENCES..111

Introduction

Religion, in some form, has existed for thousands of years. While the specific doctrines, core values, and expressions of each religion vary, they all share the belief in something beyond the material world. Although some religions put their faith in relatively simple concepts easily understood by any layperson, some religions choose to delve deeper into the mysteries surrounding the universe. Many traditional religions have offshoots studying mysticism and esotericism, dealing with the spiritual and metaphysical energy they believe exists just beyond the perceivable world.

When a group of people gets together to explore arcane and occult knowledge, they tend to be pushed to the fringes of society. Because of this, secret fraternities, brotherhoods, and organizations are often established to give those interested in these types of subjects a safe place to practice sacred rituals and share their ideas. Some of these "secret" societies are no longer hidden from plain view. The Freemasons, for example, have been plastered on the forefront of popular culture for years now, to the point where the very idea that Freemasonry could be harboring any sort of hidden agenda these days is laughable.

The Illuminati, based on the very real organization known as the Bavarian Illuminati, which was forcibly disbanded by 1787, has become a catchall for secret societies supposedly operating in the shadows. In reality, while there have been some poor attempts at resurrecting the Illuminati, they primarily exist within the realms of fiction in the form of convenient antagonists who behave cryptically and leave enigmatic clues all over for the heroes to decipher, ultimately thwarting an ill-defined plot for power. The fact remains that secret organizations from history only hid from public view because they existed during a time when any deviation from popular ideas, discourse, and religious practices could result in a death sentence for those who were caught. It was a mechanism purely driven by survival – not world domination.

Nowadays, most forms of religion or their offshoots can be practiced freely without fear of imprisonment or execution. This doesn't mean people won't ostracize or disparage someone for doing it. Still, outside of the areas where religion is strictly mandated and regulated by the state, there is little danger in publicly revealing your belief system. Things like paganism, Wicca, new age spirituality, esotericism, and mysticism have gained a significant following since the turn of the 21st century. Technology and communications have evolved to the point where it isn't very difficult to find like-minded individuals who share your interests. This is especially true for non-traditional religions and religious practices.

One of the more popular religious systems in the world today is Kabbalah. It saw exponential growth after a collection of high-profile celebrities began practicing it. However, there is a lot more to Kabbalah than someone may share on social media or talk about in red-carpet interviews. It has roots stretching back to ancient Judaism. Astrology is another form of esotericism with a prevalence in modern society. Suppose you've ever read your horoscope or looked into your zodiac sign. In that case, you will have at least a passing familiarity with it. Both Kabbalah and Astrology deeply connect to the spiritual and metaphysical side of the universe. While there are plenty of mysteries yet to uncover, learning more about them can help shine a light on some very interesting aspects of your life that you may never have known before. Anyone fascinated by the idea that you can discover your inner spirit or receive portends of the future is sure to love reading this book and learning more about it.

Chapter 1: When Kabbalah Meets Astrology

Kabbalah and astrology are both important pillars of Western esotericism. There is a rich history behind Kabbalah and its development from its inception to the modern day. Astrology has an even longer tradition among many different cultures, from ancient China, Babylon, India, Mesopotamia, and the Mayan Empire. There is a significant amount of crossover between the two practices. Astrology has an important place within Kabbalah regarding reading natal charts, studying zodiac signs, and interpreting Tarot cards. There is plenty to learn about Kabbalah and astrology and how they intermingle to comprehensively examine your personality, characteristics, ambitions, and past, present, and future.

Kabbalah has a rich history with its connection to astrology.
https://pxhere.com/en/photo/848342

What Is Kabbalah?

Kabbalah is an ancient Jewish tradition of mysticism that seeks to uncover the mysteries of God and the universe. The central teachings of Kabbalah include the concept of the Ein Sof, a divine being beyond human comprehension, and the idea that the universe is a manifestation of the Ein Sof's emanations, known as sephirot. Kabbalah strongly emphasizes studying the Zorah, or Hebrew Bible, and other sacred texts. Meditation, rituals, and prayer are used as a means to connect with the divine and gain a deeper understanding of the hidden aspects of the universe. The ultimate goal is to achieve spiritual enlightenment and a better understanding and awareness of the self.

History of Kabbalah

The history of Kabbalah can be traced back to 12th-century Spain and Southern France, particularly the region of Provence, where Jewish mystics and scholars began to explore a new understanding of Jewish theology and spirituality. These early Kabbalists drew upon earlier Jewish mystical traditions such as Merkabah and Hekhalot mysticism. They were also influenced by Neoplatonism and Gnosticism, as well as the writings of the French rabbi Isaac the Blind. Kabbalah has substantially impacted various other religious and philosophical movements, including Hasidic Judaism, Hermeticism, Christian Cabala, and Hermetic Qabalah.

A significant milestone in Kabbalah's history was the publication of the Zohar in the 13th century by Spanish rabbi and mystic Moses de León. This book is considered the foundation of Kabbalistic literature. It contains interpretations of scripture, noting instances of mysticism in the Torah, as well as content concerning mythical psychology and mythical cosmogony. It also delves into spiritual and philosophical concepts, such as God's nature, the universe's creation and structure, the essence of souls, the path to redemption, the relationship between the ego and darkness, the "true self," and the Light of God.

Kabbalah was originally a restricted work and not widely taught to the general populace of the Jewish world. However, this began to change after a series of hardships endured by the Jewish community during the Middle Ages, with the rise of antisemitism. This culminated with the Alhambra Decree (Edict of Expulsion), a joint edict issued by Isabella I of Castile and Ferdinand II of Aragon, the Catholic monarchs of Spain, which ordered all practicing Jews to vacate their kingdoms and territories in 1492. This act aimed to hamper the Jewish people's growing religious and economic influence. There was a fear that if they controlled the banks and loans, it would erode the power of the Crown. Isabella and Ferdinand also worried that many of Spain's recently-converted "New Christian" population would revert back to Judaism, diminishing the prestige and control of the Catholic Church.

Antisemitism continued to spread throughout the 16th century. As a result of the shared cultural trauma the Jewish people suffered, there was an increase in the belief that the arrival of a "Jewish Messiah" was imminent. The Jewish Messiah was entirely separate from the Christian Messiah or Jesus Christ. Still, their function in their respective religions was very similar. The Jewish populace held out hope that their Messiah would come and save them, delivering them from exile and redeeming the faithful. This form of messianism was encouraged by Jewish mystics from Safed, a small settlement in the region of Galilee, which now forms part of northern Israel.

There was a struggle for prominence within Kabbalism between the doctrine laid out in the Zohar and the tenets of the Safed mystics. The teachings of Isaac Luria, a leading rabbi and mystic from Safed, sparked the biggest transformation in Kabbalah, which adopted many of his messianic beliefs. Lurianic Kabbalism reinterpreted the Idra, which was the most esoteric section of the Zohar. It emphasized the beliefs of reincarnation, messianism, and "Tohu and Tikkun." Tohu and Tikkun depict the nature of duality, with Tohu meaning chaos and confusion, while Tikkun represents order and rectification. Luria's teachings are considered equally fundamental to Kabbalah as the Zohar.

The widespread acceptance of Kabbalah within Jewish culture saw it gain more influence on the people. In 1540, it was decided that the fundamentals of Kabbalah must be taught publicly to people of all ages. According to the Jewish mystics, only when Kabbalah had spread to the four corners of the world would violence, hatred, destruction, and war come to an end, allowing peace, harmony, and love to reign in the days leading up to the coming of the Jewish Messiah. Once this happened, time and space would shrink, while the people would learn the secrets of immortality.

Kabbalah had a major impact on the development of Hasidism. This spiritual movement endorsed the immanence of God, which taught that he was present throughout the universe. It also promoted the idea that one should strive to maintain a personal relationship with Him at all times, as well as the importance of devotion in religious practices and the spiritual significance of physical actions and daily life. In Hasidic Judaism, adherents are divided into "courts" or "dynasties," each one led by a Rebbe, who serves as their spiritual leader.

In the first half of the 18th century, "modern" Kabbalah started to take form. The Italian rabbi and philosopher Moshe Chaim Luzzatto established a "yeshiva," or a Jewish educational institution that focuses on halacha (Jewish law) and the Talmud, for the specific purpose of giving students a place to study Kabbalah. Although Luzzatto was eventually forced to close his yeshiva and turn over his writings on the subjects of Kabbalah and mysticism, his works which managed to survive, are often a starting point for people who wish to immerse themselves in the esoteric side of Judaism.

Kabbalah also significantly influenced the development of mysticism in other religions, such as Christian Cabala and Hermetic Qabalah. Christian Cabala emerged in the 16th century and adapted the beliefs of Kabbalah to Christian theology. It mainly developed among Christian scholars who studied Jewish kabbalistic texts as they sought to prove the truth of Christianity through the lens of mysticism and esoterica. Christian Cabala also emphasizes the spiritual significance of the Bible and Christian liturgy.

Hermetic Qabalah, also known as Hermeticism, emerged as a form of mysticism in the late medieval period. It is based on a syncretic blend of Kabbalah, Christian Cabala, Neoplatonism, Gnosticism, and several other spiritual and philosophical traditions. Hermetic Qabalah is often associated with the Hermetic Corpus, a group of texts from the Hellenistic period that taught Hermeticism principles. It emphasizes the study of the Tree of Life, a mystical symbol representing the path to enlightenment and the microcosm and macrocosm relationship.

At the turn of the 21st century, Kabbalah was thrust into the limelight due to several famous celebrities revealing themselves as Kabbalists. This included Madonna, Ashton Kutcher, and his then-wife, Demi Moore, Britney Spears, Gwyneth Paltrow, Paris Hilton, and Lindsay Lohan. However, many of them gave it up by the mid-2010s, as they weren't willing to devote themselves completely to religion. Instead, celebrities and those they influenced viewed Kabbalah as a shortcut to spiritual enlightenment, wielding its core tenets as a self-help weapon. Despite the celebrities and influencers losing interest in it, Kabbalah continues to be studied and practiced by many Jews and non-Jews alike. It is considered one of the most important spiritual traditions in Jewish history.

What Is Astrology?

Astrology is a belief system that holds that the positions and movements of celestial bodies, like the sun, moon, and planets, influence human behavior and the natural world. It is thought that the locations of celestial bodies at the time of a person's birth can predict certain characteristics and life events and explain aspects of their personality, relationships, and omens for the future. With its roots in ancient cultures, particularly in the Near East and the Mediterranean, astrology survives and is still widely practiced.

Astrology is the belief system that interprets the stars' effects on our lives.
ESA/Hubble, CC BY 4.0 <https://creativecommons.org/licenses/by/4.0>, via Wikimedia Commons https://commons.wikimedia.org/wiki/File:Starsinthesky.jpg

The core idea of astrology is that the universe is ordered and that the movements of the celestial bodies reflect patterns and cycles which can be understood, interpreted, and predicted. It is divided into several branches, including natal astrology, concerned with studying an individual's birth chart, and mundane astrology, which focuses on studying astrological influences on world events and large groups of people. Learning how to read charts, stars, and alignments is the first step to becoming an astrologist. It isn't always easy, but it can be incredibly rewarding once you figure it out.

It is important to note that astrology is not the same thing as astronomy, which is the study of celestial objects and phenomena that originate outside the Earth's atmosphere. Astrology isn't considered a hard scientific discipline but a pseudoscience and type of divination. Where astronomy is purely focused on what can be observed or inferred by the laws of nature, astrology deals more with psychology, emotions, and behavior. It can be difficult to definitively prove the veracity of astrology. Still, those who take it seriously and try to do it right are often pleasantly surprised by the positive results.

History of Astrology

Astrology originates in many disparate ancient civilizations, including the Mayans, Chinese, Indians, Babylonians, Egyptians, and Greeks. The Babylonians are credited with developing the first system of astrology around 2,400 BCE, which they used primarily for predicting eclipses and other celestial events. The first text to describe astrology appeared around 1,400 BCE in the Indian subcontinent and was called the Vedanga Jyotisha. The Mayans had their own form of astrology, using the stars to determine different signs and track the passage of time on their infamous calendar. The Mayan year was only 260 days, divided into 13 galactic numbers (similar to months), with 20 days in each galactic number.

In ancient Egypt, astrology was closely tied to religious beliefs and was used to predict the fate of the pharaohs and the kingdom. The Egyptians also developed a form of horoscopic astrology, which uses the position of the sun, moon, and planets at the time of a person's birth to make predictions about their future. The ancient Greek version of astrology was influenced by the works of philosophers such as Pythagoras and Plato, who believed in the connection between the celestial realm and the human world. The Greek system of astrology was later adopted by the Romans, who spread it throughout their empire.

Astrology was widely accepted as a legitimate discipline in Europe during the Middle Ages. Monarchs often used it to make decisions about state affairs. It also played a role in the development of modern astronomy, as many early astronomers were also astrologers. However, during the scientific revolution of the 16th and 17th centuries, astrology lost ground as a science, as it was found to be unable to provide reliable predictions, which many wrote off as akin to superstition. Today astrology is mainly used for self-help, entertainment, and self-exploration.

Kabbalah, Astrology, and Western Esotericism

Kabbalah, astrology, and western esotericism are all forms of spiritual and mystical thought seeking to explore hidden knowledge, understand the influence of celestial bodies, and aim for spiritual enlightenment. While the three share some commonalities and can be practiced together, each has its own specific teachings and traditions with distinct differences. Kabbalah is more focused on God and the universe, especially with the prominence of sacred texts documenting the history of the Jewish people. Astrology is primarily concerned with the movements of celestial bodies, their positions relative to one another, and how these can influence human affairs and the natural world. Western esotericism encompasses a broad range of mystical and spiritual traditions and experienced its development within Western societies, including practices like Rosicrucianism, hermeticism, alchemy, and theosophy.

Kabbalistic Calendar

The Kabbalistic calendar is a unique calendar that's separate from the Gregorian calendar. It's based on the cycle of lunar months, and as with all calendars centered on the moon's phases, there are times when it will lag behind, necessitating the addition of temporary months. Because this calendar was specifically designed for Kabbalah, it allows individuals to align their spiritual practices, rituals, and mystical beliefs with the universe's energies. According to Kabbalah, certain days and times are more conducive to specific aspects of these customs, so its calendar lets individuals identify those days and times.

The Kabbalah calendar is divided into four phases that correspond to the four worlds of Kabbalah: Atzilut, Beriah, Yetzirah, and Asiyah. Each phase is connected to a different stage in the spiritual journey and is associated with distinctive spiritual practices. It is divided into 72 weeks, with each week correlated with a specific sephirah, or attribute, of God.

Each week is associated with a certain custom or meditation, assisting in their spiritual alignment. It's important to note that the Kabbalah calendar is not widely used by traditional Jewish communities and is considered part of modern Kabbalah scholarship, as opposed to the original interpretation. Although the traditional Jewish calendar is also based on lunar cycles, the calendar specifically tied to Kabbalah is rejected by many leaders within Judaism.

How the Kabbalistic Calendar Works

The days in the Kabbalistic calendar are each considered positive, negative, or neutral days. Positive days possess abundant energy and are ideal for starting new projects like getting married, purchasing a new home, planting seeds in a garden, or embarking on a new business venture. The days particularly strong with positive energy are the first days of each month, which coincide with the new moons. Starting the month by taking advantage of the first day's positive energy can extend that energy to the entire month.

Negative days lack energy, which makes them the opposite of positive days. Things in your life initiated on negative days have a greater chance of failure since the entire venture will be imbued with negative energy. Neutral days don't have more or less energy, remaining entirely balanced between the two sides. You can start a venture on a neutral day and still see success, but it will be more difficult than if you did so on a positive day. Conversely, your chances of experiencing failure will be less than if you started it on a negative day.

The Jewish Holy Day, known as Shabbat, begins at sundown every Friday and ends at sunset on Saturday. Kabbalists believe that Shabbat is the only day of the week when the spiritual and physical realms align, boosting the amount of positive energy during this period. The flow of spiritual energy is also heightened during Shabbat, making it available for personal connections and individual growth. Shabbat allows practitioners to access a higher level of their souls and change their destinies for the upcoming week.

Holidays celebrated during the Jewish year are not just about tradition. They are imbued with a lot of positive energy, making them powerful tools for personal growth and improvement. These holidays serve as cosmic portals in time that allow for connection to various frequencies of positive spiritual energy, which can help eliminate negativity and chaos, leading to increased fulfillment in life. Each holiday offers a unique channel to access this spiritual energy and learn how to grow as a person.

Months of the Kabbalistic Calendar

- **Nisan:** This is the 1st month by the ecclesiastical reckoning and the 7th month (8th during leap years) by the civil reckoning of the Kabbalistic calendar. Nisan contains 30 days. It is roughly the equivalent of March to April in the Gregorian calendar. Major Jewish holidays which fall within Nisan include Passover and Akitu.

- **Iyar:** This is the 2nd month by the ecclesiastical reckoning and the 8th month (9th during leap years) by the civil reckoning of the Kabbalistic calendar. Iyar contains 29 days. It is roughly the equivalent of April to May in the Gregorian calendar. Pesach Sheni and Lag Baomer are celebrated during this month.

- **Sivan:** This is the 3rd month by the ecclesiastical reckoning and the 9th month (10th during leap years) by the civil reckoning of the Kabbalistic calendar. Sivan contains 30 days. It is roughly the equivalent of May to June in the Gregorian calendar. The Jewish holiday of Shavuot is celebrated within Sivan.

- **Tammuz:** This is the 4th month by the ecclesiastical reckoning and the 10th month (11th during leap years) by the civil reckoning of the Kabbalistic calendar. Tammuz contains 29 days. It is roughly the equivalent of June to July in the Gregorian calendar. The fast day known as the Seventeenth of Tammuz falls within this month.

- **Av:** This is the 5th month by the ecclesiastical reckoning and the 11th month (12th during leap years) by the civil reckoning of the Kabbalistic calendar. Av contains 30 days. It is roughly the equivalent of July to August in the Gregorian calendar. The Jewish holidays of Tisha B'Av and Tu B'Av are celebrated during Av.

- **Elul:** This is the 6th month by the ecclesiastical reckoning and the 12th month (13th during leap years) by the civil reckoning of the Kabbalistic calendar. Elul contains 29 days. It is roughly the equivalent of August to September in the Gregorian calendar. Elul is traditionally a month of repentance undertaken in preparation for the High Holy Days during Tishrei.

- **Tishrei:** This is the 7th month by the ecclesiastical reckoning and the 1st month by the civil reckoning of the Kabbalistic calendar. Tishrei contains 30 days. It is roughly the equivalent of September to October in the Gregorian calendar. In addition to celebrating the Jewish New Year, major Jewish holidays falling within Tishrei include the High Holy Days of Rosh Hashanah and Yom Kippur.

- **Cheshvan:** This is the 8th month by the ecclesiastical reckoning and the 2nd month by the civil reckoning of the Kabbalistic calendar. Cheshvan contains 29 or 30 days, depending on whether or not Rosh Hashanah is postponed that year. It is roughly the equivalent of October to November in the Gregorian calendar. Marcheshvan and the Fast of Behav fall within Cheshvan.

- **Kislev:** This is the 9th month by the ecclesiastical reckoning and the 3rd month by the civil reckoning of the Kabbalistic calendar. Kislev contains 29 or 30 days, depending on whether or not Rosh Hashanah is postponed that year. It is roughly the equivalent of November to December in the Gregorian calendar. The major Jewish holiday of Hanukkah falls within Kislev.

- **Tevet:** This is the 10th month by the ecclesiastical reckoning and the 4th month by the civil reckoning of the Kabbalistic calendar. Tevet contains 29 days. It is roughly the equivalent of December to January in the Gregorian calendar. If Kislev is short, Hanukkah will end in Tevet. The fast day known as the Tenth of Tevet also falls within this month.

- **Shevat:** This is the 11th month by the ecclesiastical reckoning and the 5th month by the civil reckoning of the Kabbalistic calendar. Shevat contains 30 days. It is roughly the equivalent of January to February in the Gregorian calendar. Tu Bishvat, a Jewish holiday celebrating the renewal of the trees, falls within Shevat.

- **Adar:** This is the 12th month by the ecclesiastical reckoning and the 6th month by the civil reckoning of the Kabbalistic calendar. Adar contains 29 days. It is roughly the equivalent of February to March in the Gregorian calendar. During leap years, Shevat is followed by Adar Aleph or Adar I, a 30-day intercalary month. Adar Aleph is then followed by this month, called Adar Bet or Adar II. Major Jewish holidays that fall within this month include Purim, the Feast of Esther, and the fast day known as the Seventh of Adar, which honors the death of Moses.

Kabbalistic vs. Gregorian Calendars

Although there are some crossovers and similarities between the Kabbalistic and Gregorian calendars, some key differences set them apart. The Gregorian calendar is based on solar cycles for establishing the months and years, while the Kabbalistic calendar is lunar-based. Most of the principal calendars worldwide are lunar calendars, with only the Julian and Gregorian calendars using solar years. The Gregorian calendar is the primary one used in Western civilizations, so it is often the calendar with which most people in the West are familiar. It makes no attempt to synchronize with the moon's cycles, despite the prevalence of lunar-based calendars throughout the rest of the world.

The Gregorian calendar is synchronized with one full revolution around the sun, which takes approximately 365.2422 days. Most years possess 365 days, with months containing either 30 or 31 days, except for February, which has 28. To account for the extra fraction of a day and realign the calendar year with the Earth's revolution around the sun, a "leap day" is added to the end of February every 4 years, known as "leap years." However, the calendar will still be slightly off after a century or so. To remedy this, every year exactly divisible by 100 will not be a leap year, but centurial years that can be divided by 400 *exactly* will be leap years. This means the years 1700, 1800, and 1900 were not leap years, but 2000 was a leap year.

Meanwhile, the Kabbalistic calendar will almost always have a new month that coincides with a new moon and lasts until the end of the lunar cycle. The Kabbalistic calendar will sometimes add a 13th month to a particular year to account for the discrepancies built up over several years due to the months synching to the lunar cycle instead of the solar cycle. This normally occurs every 2 to 3 years over a 19-year cycle, with seven leap years during the cycle. The additional month is placed between Shevat and Adar, the 11th and 12th months, respectively, by the ecclesiastical reckoning. It essentially splits Adar into two months, the first containing 30 days and the second having the usual 29 days.

The extra months are marked by an epithet of the first two letters from the Hebrew alphabet, "Aleph" and "Bet," or simply by adding the Roman numerals of "I" and "II" to the end of Adar. Part of the reason for synching the Kabbalistic calendar with the solar calendar is to ensure that the Jewish holidays also remain synchronized with the Gregorian calendar. This makes it easier for those who practice Kabbalah and Judaism in general while living in the Western world to celebrate their major holidays at approximately the same time every year.

The leap years of the Kabbalistic calendar are determined by the Metonic cycle, which is based on the fact that there are roughly 235 lunar months in 19 solar years. The years 3, 6, 8, 11, 14, 17, and 19 within the 19-year cycle are leap years. To determine whether a Kabbalistic year is a leap year, find its position within the 19-year Metonic cycle. This position is calculated by dividing the Kabbalistic year number by 19 and finding the remainder. For example, if the Kabbalistic year 5782 (the equivalent of the year 2022 CE in the Gregorian calendar) is divided by 19, it results in a remainder of 6, indicating that it is a leap year. Note that there is no year 0 in the Jewish calendar, so a remainder of 0 means that the year is the 19th of the Metonic cycle, which is a leap year.

Another difference from the Gregorian calendar is that the Kabbalistic calendar can add or subtract days to prevent major Jewish holidays like Rosh Hashana from falling on certain days of the week. A day can be added to Cheshvan, the 8th month, or it can be subtracted from Kislev, the 9th month. Ultimately, these adjustments result in any given year in the Kabbalistic calendar can have 6 different lengths. Common years can have 353, 354, or 355, while leap years can have 383, 384, or 385 days. Years with 353 or 383 days are known as deficient years; years with 354 or 384 are known as regular years; and years with 355 or 385 days are known as complete years.

Kabbalistic and Astrological Principles

Kabbalistic astrology uses chart readings – just like in other forms of astrology – to aid in self-discovery, realizing your potential, and improving your ability to communicate and express your ideas, visions, and emotions. It can also help you understand how to interact effectively with others. Each person is born with unique talents and challenges associated with their astrological sign. These signs serve as guides, highlighting problems that must be overcome and identifying your purpose in life. The ultimate goal of kabbalistic astrology is to transcend the effects of the universe and assert control over your own life.

The Zodiac signs do not determine your personality traits so much as your personality dictates your sign. The karma acquired in a previous life determines which sign you need to be born under to gain the attributes and characteristics necessary to correct past mistakes, find personal growth, and improve yourself into a better version of yourself. Ideally, you will eventually reach the point where you have become your best self, which means you can find oneness with God. This is a critical point to the teachings of Kabbalah, especially as it was laid out by the patriarch Abraham around 3,800 years ago in the text called Sefer Yetzirah, the Book of Formation. Abraham is considered Kabbalah's very first astrologer.

The biggest difference between Kabbalistic astrology and other forms of astrology is that the former uses a lunar calendar, and the latter tends to use solar calendars, particularly the Gregorian calendar. While the names for the Zodiac in Kabbalah remain the same, each sign corresponds to a single Kabbalistic month rather than being split across two months like it is with the Gregorian calendar. The Kabbalastic months and their Zodiac signs are as follows:

- **Aries (Nisan):** The Ram (Hebrew Name: Taleh)
- **Taurus (Iyar):** The Bull (Hebrew Name: Shor)
- **Gemini (Sivan):** The Twins (Hebrew Name: Teomim)
- **Cancer (Tammuz):** The Crab (Hebrew Name: Sartan)
- **Leo (Av):** The Lion (Hebrew Name: Aryeh)
- **Virgo (Elul):** The Virgin (Hebrew Name: Betulah)
- **Libra (Tishrei):** The Scales (Hebrew Name: Moznaim)
- **Scorpio (Cheshvan):** The Scorpion (Hebrew Name: 'Akrav)
- **Sagittarius (Kislev):** The Archer (Hebrew Name: Kashat)
- **Capricorn (Tevet):** The Goat (Hebrew Name: G'di)
- **Aquarius (Shevat):** The Water-Bearer (Hebrew Name: D'li)
- **Pisces (Adar I and Adar II):** The Fish (Hebrew Name: Dagim)

The Role of Kabbalistic Astrology in Tarot Reading

Kabbalistic astrology plays an important role in Tarot reading, providing a framework for interpreting the meanings and symbolism of Tarot cards. Kabbalah, as an ancient Jewish mystical tradition, focuses on the spiritual aspects of the universe and the connection between God, humanity, and the world. Since it teaches that everything in the universe is interconnected, Tarot cards can be used to understand and access the hidden wisdom of the universe. It provides a spiritual and mystical perspective on the Tarot deck and helps uncover the hidden wisdom and insights the Tarot cards can offer.

In Tarot reading, the approach using Kabbalistic astrology offers an understanding of how the Tree of Life, a major Kabbalistic symbol, relates to the universe's structure. The Tree of Life consists of ten sephirot, or emanations, which correspond to the major arcana cards of the Tarot. The sephirot represent different aspects of the universe and the human experience, which can be used to understand the deeper meanings of the Tarot cards. Kabbalah also teaches the concept of the "Ein Sof," God's infinite and unknowable aspect. This connects to the "Unknowable" cards in Tarot, like the High Priestess and the Hermit.

Chapter 2: The Kabbalistic Tree of Life

The Kabbalistic Tree of Life is well-known for its mystical powers and insight. It has long been a part of the traditions of Kabbalah, stemming back to professor and philosopher Paolo Riccio's 1516 CE Latin translation of Gates of Light, written by Spanish Kabbalist Joseph Gikatilla. The earliest modern incarnation of the Kabbalistic Tree of Life was designed by the German scholar Johann Reuchlin, although this version lacked the full array of possible paths between the spheres. Reuchlin's design appeared on the cover of Gates of Light; later, Kabbalists would increase the original 17 paths within the Tree of Life to 21 or 22 paths. In the late 1600s, German Kabbalist Christian Knorr von Rosenroth wrote and published Kabbala Denudat, in which he introduced an updated version of the Tree of Life that had 11 spheres to complement the 22 paths for the first time.

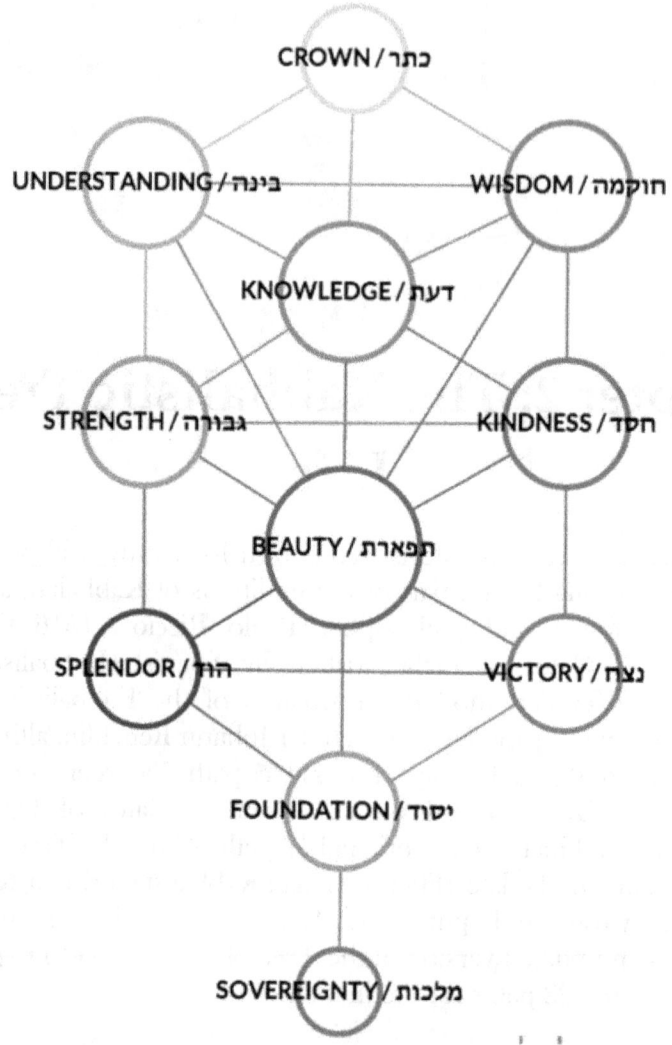

A simplified version of the Kabbalistic Tree of Life.
Ideasfisherman, CC BY-SA 3.0 <https://creativecommons.org/licenses/by-sa/3.0>, via Wikimedia Commons https://commons.wikimedia.org/wiki/File:Kabbalahtree.png

Additional updates of the diagram continued throughout the 18th and 19th centuries, but there were still several distinct versions that placed the individual nodes in different positions. Part of this was due to the discovery of new planets in the solar system. Originally, most of the Tree of Life designs only contained Mercury through Uranus. Still, after Neptune and Pluto were confirmed to exist, these were included in updated versions while preserving the 22 paths of older designs. By the 21st century, the Kabbalistic Tree of Life had a relatively consistent design used by most sources. When Pluto was downgraded from a planet to a dwarf planet in August 2006, this, fortunately, did not affect the Tree of Life since the most commonly used design already positioned it as a "hidden sphere," so nothing needed to be changed to accommodate its adjusted status.

What Is the Tree of Life?

The Kabbalistic Tree of Life is a mystical diagram of interconnected nodes based on the traditional Jewish Tree of Life that serves as a major symbol within Kabbalah. It represents the structure of the universe and the path to enlightenment, offering multiple possible avenues to achieve them. The Tree comprises ten spheres, or sephirot, which are connected by 22 paths. Each sephirah represents a different aspect of God and the universe, and the paths between them symbolize the soul's journey to enlightenment. The tree is also seen as a map of the soul itself and the quest of the individual's attempt to connect with the divine.

The Tree of Life visually represents the universe's superior and inferior dimensions. It illustrates the concept that everything outside of us also exists within us, and the Tree of Life is a prime example of a macrocosm existing within a microcosm. It guides people to awaken their higher consciousness and return to where they originated, illustrating the microcosm. The Tree also represents the potential for humanity to do the same, which would be the macrocosm. The Tree of Life is derived from the manifestations known as the Ain, the Limitless, and the Absolute. The flow of celestial forces into the act of creation is what shapes and forms each sephirah. Just as water will spill from one tier of a fountain to the next, each sephiroth becomes denser than the one which came before it and has more rules and boundaries.

Role in the Macrocosm

In the Kabbalistic Tree of Life, the macrocosm is the overall result of every sephiroth and path working in unison toward a shared goal. Just as each sphere is an individual piece of a larger puzzle, every person who has ever lived was created in the image of God, but they lack the knowledge and power of God. Only when a person transcends their individualistic nature and rejoins God as a part of the whole do they become a fully-realized piece of the divine. This is also depicted in how the individual planets comprise the solar system. Zooming out farther, the planets of our solar system revolve around the sun, which is merely one star in a galaxy filled with stars. Taking it one more step beyond, our galaxy is one of *many galaxies* across the known universe.

Role in the Microcosm

The microcosm in the Kabbalistic Tree of Life is represented by the individual sephirah, with each one possessing certain characteristics and traits that feed into the Tree as a whole. The sephirot ultimately work together, connected by the 22 paths, to achieve the shared goal of harmonic relations to Creation and the universe. Each planet has its own environment and ecosystems, but the only one teeming with life is the Earth. All the people and their cities, towns, countries, and continents make up the whole of the Earth and serve as a microcosm of the larger universe. Zooming in more, you can view each individual as possessing their own microcosm of a universe within themselves, especially regarding the vast and uncharted seas of the mind, body, and soul.

Connection to Sacred Geometry

Sacred geometry is the belief that there are geometric shapes and proportions which can be assigned divine meaning. These sacred shapes and proportions prove that God is the Creator of the universe since it would be impossible for a purely random and self-perpetuating universe to possess these types of designs. Many mathematical forms can be observed in nature, either through their geometric patterns or behaviors. Because of this, the Kabbalist viewpoint is that it must have been created deliberately, and the Creator must be God. These beliefs are borne out in the structure and purpose of the Tree of Life.

Sacred geometry is shapes that are assigned divine meanings.
Violetcabra, CC0, via Wikimedia Commons
https://commons.wikimedia.org/wiki/File:Sacred_Geometry_Construction_with_Color.jpg

The Four Worlds of Kabbalah

The Four Worlds of Kabbalah are the realms of spiritual essence and emanation, including a descending chain of Existence. They are named Atziluth, Beriah, Yetzirah, and Assiah. Each realm with the Four Worlds design sits at a different level and has its own functions within the Kabbalistic cosmology. The Four Worlds are believed to have been imbued with the creative life force of Ein Sof, also called the Divine Creator or God. However, the Four Worlds don't only refer to their position within the universe or their role in its creation – they can also represent the levels of consciousness that exist in the human psyche or experience.

Atziluth

Atziluth is the first and highest realm of the Four Worlds. Other names for it include the World of Emanations or the World of Causes. It manifests within the top three sephirot in the Tree of Life. The realm of Atziluth is considered eternal, representing pure divinity, and is connected to the emanation of God's essence, or the free act of the will of God. The sephirot of Atziluth are an expression of the closeness of this realm in proximity to the Creator. All of creation is considered to spring from this realm, originating everything that has been, is, or ever will be. It is identified with the element of fire.

Beriah

Beriah is the second realm of the Four Worlds, the next one down from Atziluth. The other name for it is the World of Creation. It is associated with the sephirot of wisdom and understanding. Beriah works in conjunction with the realm above it, as it is where the ideas and concepts of Atziluth are given their form and tangible expression. This is the realm of the divine intellect and is purported to be the source of the archangels and spiritual realms. Beriah is also considered the realm of pure thought, where the sephirot remain in their purest form but are now being used to create and sustain the universe. Unlike Atziluth, which is eternal and made by the emanation of God, Beriah was created with a definitive point of origin. It is identified with the element of air.

Yetzirah

Yetzirah is the third realm of the Four Worlds and sits below Beriah. The other name for it is the World of Formation. It is associated with the middle sephirot of the Tree of Life, representing love, kindness, and justice. This is where the ideas and concepts of Beriah are given their shape and structure. The realm is split into two halves: "half good" and "half evil." The half-good manifests as emotional sensitivity and the desire to make others happy, while the half-evil is seen as a being's self-consciousness and negative emotions. It gave the creations of God a more concrete form and helped to organize the layout of the universe. Yetzirah is where the lesser angels and stars originate, as well as the place where the souls of human beings can interact with the spiritual world and seek passage to the higher realms. It is identified with the element of water.

Assiah

Assiah is the fourth and lowest realm of the Four Worlds. The other name for it is the World of Action. This is where the ideas and concepts coalesced within Yetzirah are given solid form and manifestation. It is the source of the material world and the physical universe. Assiah is associated with the sephirot of power and foundation, where the attributes of God are completely hidden, and His creations have become entirely independent from Him. Human beings dwell here and interact with the physical world, where their ultimate goal is to immerse themselves in spiritual practice to elevate their souls from Assiah to the higher realms.

The Seven Chakras

The word "chakra" translates to "wheel," referring to areas on your body that contain a significant amount of complex points of spiritual energy. They are likened to disks of energy constantly spinning and needing to remain open and aligned. Chakras are an ancient system that first developed in India around 1500 to 1000 BCE. Their first mention came in the Vedas, a collection of sacred texts of spiritual learning written during this same period of antiquity.

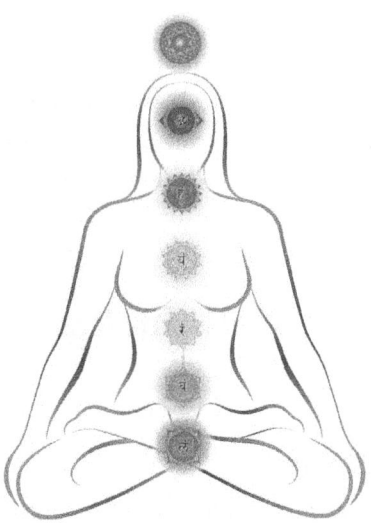

Each chakra corresponds to major organs and nerves that affect your spiritual and physical well-being.

RootOfAllLight, CC BY-SA 4.0 <https://creativecommons.org/licenses/by-sa/4.0>, via Wikimedia Commons https://commons.wikimedia.org/wiki/File:7ChakrasFemale.png

Each chakra point corresponds to collections of nerves and major organs around your body that influence your physical, emotional, and spiritual health. While there are as many as 114 different chakras, the seven primary chakras run along your spine and have the greatest effect on you. Each individual chakra can resonate with people at different times. Certain chakras may be a continuous source of blockages for some, while these blockages may be temporary for others. In the chakra system, these patterns have specific terms and recommended treatments. The seven primary chakras each have a name, number, color, and specific location along your spine that is connected to them.

Root Chakra

Number: 1
Kabbalistic Name: Yesod
Area: Base of the spine
Represents: Personality, balance, and tradition
Color: Red

The root chakra, or *Muladhara* in Sanskrit, is the first of the seven chakras. It is located at the base of the spine and represents the foundation of your being, being closely linked to your survival instincts, physical identity, and grounding to the earth. You will feel safe, stable, and secure when your root chakra is open and balanced. You'll also feel a sense of belonging and connectedness to your physical body and the world around you. On the other hand, when your root chakra is blocked or imbalanced, you might feel listless, anxious, or disconnected from your physical body. Symptoms of a blocked root chakra include fatigue, muscle pain, and lower back pain.

Sacral Chakra

Number: 2
Kabbalistic Name: Hod-Nezah
Area: Below the belly button
Represents: Satisfaction, creativity, and pleasure
Color: Orange

The sacral chakra, also known as *Svadhishthana* in Sanskrit, is the second of the seven chakras. It is located in the lower abdomen, just below the navel, and represents your emotional and creative energy. This chakra is also associated with the feeling of pleasure and romantic pursuits. When the sacral chakra is open and balanced, you will feel emotionally stable and open to new experiences. You may feel a sense of creativity and healthy romantic energy. If the sacral chakra is blocked or imbalanced, you can become emotionally unstable, have difficulty with boundaries, or possess a low libido. Symptoms of an imbalanced sacral chakra may include lower back pain, hip pain, and romantic dysfunction.

Solar Plexus Chakra

Number: 3
Kabbalistic Name: Tiferet
Area: Upper abdomen
Represents: Confidence and self-worth
Color: Yellow

The solar plexus chakra, also known as Manipura in Sanskrit, is the third of the seven chakras. It is located in the abdomen, above the navel. This chakra has a strong association with the element of fire. The solar plexus chakra governs your personal power, will, and self-esteem. When it is open and balanced, you will be more confident, possess a sense of purpose, have more self-control, and maintain a positive self-image. A blocked or imbalanced solar plexus chakra can manifest as feelings of powerlessness, a lack of self-worth, and difficulty when making important decisions. Blockages can cause digestive issues, including heartburn, indigestion, ulcers, and eating disorders.

Heart Chakra

Number: 4

Kabbalistic Name: Gevurah-Hesed

Area: Center of the chest

Represents: Love, empathy, and mercy

Color: Green

The heart chakra, also known as Anahata in Sanskrit, is the fourth of the seven chakras. It is located in the center of the chest, directly above the heart. This chakra governs emotions such as love, compassion, mercy, and self-acceptance. An open and balanced heart chakra allows you to connect with others, feeling a strong sense of affection, appreciation, and acceptance. When it is blocked or imbalanced, you could experience physical or emotional issues related to your heart and circulatory system. It can also affect your relationships, creating difficulties between you and others and harming your emotional well-being. Some practices used to balance the heart chakra include meditation, yoga, and energy healing.

Throat Chakra

Number: 5

Kabbalistic Name: Da'at

Area: The throat

Represents: Communication and instruction

Color: Blue

The throat chakra, also known as Vishuddhi in Sanskrit, is the fifth of the seven chakras. It is located within your throat and the surrounding area. This chakra controls your ability to communicate and impart knowledge to others. It governs your thyroid gland, vocal cords, mouth, and ears. When the throat chakra is open and balanced, you will have an easier time verbalizing your point of view, making your feelings clear, and listening with compassion and understanding. Your confidence will shine through because you can speak your truth. When it is blocked or imbalanced, you might find it difficult to express yourself or feel heard, and you are less likely to listen or comprehend what others are trying to tell you. Physical symptoms of a blocked throat chakra include health issues such as a sore throat or thyroid issues.

Third Eye Chakra

Number: 6

Kabbalistic Name: Binah-Hokhmah

Area: Between the eyes on the forehead

Represents: Perception, innate knowledge, and imagination

Color: Indigo

The third eye chakra, also known as Ajna in Sanskrit, is the sixth of the seven chakras. It is located in the center of the forehead, between the eyebrows, and is often depicted as a purple or indigo lotus flower with two petals. This chakra is associated with intuition, wisdom, and spiritual insight. It governs your pituitary gland, pineal gland, eyes, and brain. When the third eye chakra is open and balanced, you will have a strong intuition, the ability to think clearly, and a deep sense of inner knowing. When it is blocked or imbalanced, it can manifest as confusion, lack of direction, and difficulty in making decisions. Physical symptoms due to a blockage include headaches, sinus issues, or eye problems.

Crown Chakra

Number: 7

Kabbalistic Name: Keter

Area: Top of the head

Represents: Consciousness and mental acumen

Color: White or violet

The crown chakra, also known as Sahasrara in Sanskrit, is the seventh of the seven chakras. It is located at the very top of your head and has a connection to all the other chakras and their corresponding organs in your body, including your brain and nervous system. This chakra represents the connection of your physical form to your spiritual purpose and enlightenment. When your crown chakra is open and balanced, it can help keep all the other chakras open, bringing you a sense of inner peace and spiritual fulfillment. However, if this chakra is blocked or imbalanced, you may appear to be closed-minded, skeptical, or inflexible.

The Sephirot

Sephirot (singular: sephirah) are defined as emanations through which Ein Sof and the infinite are revealed. They are constantly creating the physical realm and the higher metaphysical realms of the Four Worlds. The sephirot are arranged in multiple levels within the Tree of Life, representing where their corresponding realms are positioned within the hierarchy of the universe. There are ten regular sephirot within the Tree of Life and one elevated sephirah, organized in a descending chain from heaven to earth, like the Four Worlds. Their names and numbers are: 0-Kether, 1-Chokmah, 2-Binah, 3-Da'at, 4-Chesed, 5-Geburah, 6-Tiferet, 7-Netsach, 8-Hod, 9-Yesod, and 10-Malkuth.

The Tree of Life and the Seven Chakras

0. Keter is the highest of the sephirot, also known as *Crown*, and is positioned above all the others. It is labeled as "superconsciousness" and is an eternal state of being an infinite source of creation. There is no limit to the potential of what is conceived and produced here, as well as producing a never-ending number of possibilities. It is the ultimate metaphysical reality, represented by the color gold. This sephirah denotes purification, flexibility, and conductivity.
1. Chochmah is part of the Intellectual Triad or Supernal Triangle found beneath Keter and is also known as Wisdom. It is the sephirah of insight, intuition, inspiration, unformed awareness, and a germinating idea. Chochmah embodies the emergence of something from nothing, represented by the color navy blue.
2. Binah is part of the Intellectual Triad or Supernal Triangle, also known as Understanding. It is the sephirah that expresses the expansion of an idea, the plotting of a story, and the establishment of the structure. Binah depicts the formation of concepts and matter, represented by the color dark red.

3. Da'at is part of the Intellectual Triad or Supernal Triangle and is also known as Knowing. It is the sephirah showing the identification and integration of ideas, creating an intimate connection between them and the divine. Da'at depicts the naming and application of that which is creation, represented by the color gray.
4. Chesed is part of the Emotional Triad and Ethical Triangle, found beneath the Intellectual Triad, and is also known as Unbounded Love. The sephirah expands ideas, widens their sphere of influence, and expresses empathy. Chesed depicts personal growth and concern for others, represented by the color blue.
5. Geburah is part of the Emotional Triad or Ethical Triangle, also known as Strength of Boundaries. It is the sephirah that encourages the setting of limits, communicating refusal, and looking for focus. Geburah depicts the establishment of strong boundaries, represented by the color red.
6. Tiferet is part of the Emotional Triad or Ethical Triangle, also known as Beauty. It is the sephirah that synchronizes opposing energies and shows compassion to others. Tiferet depicts harmony and kindness, represented by the color yellow.
7. Netsach is part of the Instinctual Triad and Magical Triangle, found beneath the Emotional Triad and known as Victory. It is the sephirah that helps in breaking down barriers, overcoming hardships, and managing intentions. Netsach depicts beating the odds and conquering obstacles, represented by the color purple.
8. Hod is part of the Instinctual Triad and Magical Triangle, also known as Surrender. It is the sephirah that encourages acceptance, capitulation, and acknowledgment of limitations. Hod depicts knowing when to give up and allowing things to happen on their own, represented by the color orange.
9. Yesod is part of the Instinctual Triad and Magical Triangle, also known as Foundation. It is the sephirah involved in telling the truth, discerning lies, and trustworthiness. Yesod depicts honesty, authenticity, and diligence, represented by the color green.

10. Malkuth is the lowest of the sephirot, also known as Sovereignty. It is the final stop on the Tree of Life, as the energy flow from Keter through the pathways culminates in Malkuth. This involves transforming from an abstract idea, concept, or matter to a *concrete expression* of these things. Malkuth is what manifests at the end of the journey or the actualized expression of the path, represented by the color brown.

The Kabbalistic Paths

The Kabbalistic Tree of Life contains a total of 32 possible mystical paths to discovering the secret wisdom imparted by the emanations of Ein Sof. These mystical paths include the 10 sephirot and the 22 Hebrew letter paths between them that connect everything together. In order to fully realize the meaning of the Tree of Life and its divine power, you must carefully study the sephirot and their Hebrew letter paths, discerning how they fit together. There is a strong correlation between the Hebrew alphabet and the spiritual energy of the sephirot, giving the Hebrew letters a mystical connotation within the Tree of Life.

Divine Language

Kabbalah is considered one of the four divine languages used in the Torah, with the others being Aggadah, Halachah, and Tanach. Human beings can achieve the capability to communicate with God through the use of divine languages. The actions of Moses are seen as an ideal example of discovering the ability to speak with the Divine Creator, and it is believed that all those who follow in his footsteps can eventually learn to do the same. Unlike the other divine languages, Kabbalah also contains a mystical aspect, hiding esoteric secrets that must be studied closely for many years before you can engage with them. Practitioners maintain that the letters and words of the Hebrew alphabet possess mystical qualities, and these properties can be wielded to unlock the occult knowledge connected to the divine.

The Hebrew Alphabet

The Sefer Yetzirah, written by Abraham 3,800 years ago, suggests that the letters of the Hebrew alphabet serve as the building blocks of the universe, embodying the divine energy of the Creator and the intelligence behind His creations. This includes every planet, moon, star, galaxy, and other cosmic phenomenon. Each month is associated with both a sign of the zodiac and a planet, the moon, or the sun. They are also all linked to a specific letter from the Hebrew alphabet. According to the Book of Formation, meditation exercises on the Hebrew letter connected to the current month can positively influence the events that occur during the month.

The 22 Hebrew Letter Paths

The 22 paths marked with letters from the Hebrew alphabet that connect the sephirot of the Tree of Life each have a specific meaning and mystical power.

א **Aleph:** The first letter of the Hebrew alphabet. It means "oneness with God," being a symbol of unity and the origin point from which all creation arises. This letter is associated with the concept of Divine Nothingness, as well as Ein Sof, which represents God's infinite and unknowable nature. Aleph is also the first letter in the three words used for the mystical name of God - אהיה אשר אהיה, pronounced as 'ehye 'ăšer 'ehye (Hebrew is read from right to left) - a translation of the phrase "I Am who I Am," which was the answer given to Moses in the Book of Exodus when he asked for God's true name.

ב **Bet:** The second letter of the Hebrew alphabet. It is associated with the concept of Binah, the third sephirah on the Tree of Life. This letter can be considered the feminine aspect of the divine, sometimes called the "Great Mother" or "Great Sea," and it has a connection with intellect and understanding. Bet also represents the ability to discern and differentiate between different matters and ideas, bringing a sense of cohesion or binding to the origins of creation. It symbolizes the foundation of the universe and the force known as the Divine Will, which brings everything into existence.

ג **Gimel:** The third letter of the Hebrew alphabet. It evokes Chesed, the fourth sephirah on the Tree of Life. This letter possesses the attributes of love, kindness, and compassion, considered to be the source of all benevolence and positive actions. Gimel symbolizes God's grace and generosity and an association with the concepts of endowment and energy flow. Universal abundance and prosperity originate from the attributes of Gimel, which is also the source of all blessings and generosity in the world.

ד **Dalet:** The fourth letter of the Hebrew alphabet. It is connected to Geburah, the fifth sephirah on the Tree of Life. This letter possesses the attributes of strength, discipline, and judgment, being considered the source of all boundaries, laws, and limitations. Dalet can also be referred to as the Might or Power, expressing the justice of God. The idea of control and restriction is imbued in Dalet, representing the origin of structure and order within the universe. It symbolizes Divine Justice, embodying the concepts of fairness and righteousness.

ה **He:** The fifth letter of the Hebrew alphabet. It is associated with Tiferet, the sixth sephirah on the Tree of Life. This letter contains the attributes of balance, harmony, and beauty, the origin of all integration and balance in the universe. It is called the Glory or Beauty, expressing God's compassion and mercy. He is connected to the idea of Divine Compassion, from which compassion and beauty spring forth throughout the world.

ו **Vav:** The sixth letter of the Hebrew alphabet. It is linked to Netsach, the seventh sephirah on the Tree of Life. This letter has the characteristics of victory, endurance, and persistence and is the source of all-natural instincts and processes. Vav can be viewed as the Eternity or Victory, connected to the idea of an eternal and enduring God. It is also known as Divine Endurance, serving as the root of the world's victories and perseverance.

ז **Zayin:** The seventh letter of the Hebrew alphabet. It connects with Hod, the eighth sephirah on the Tree of Life. This letter symbolizes humility, surrender, and giving thanks. Submission and surrendering to God's will are major components of Zayin. It also has connotations of splendor, majesty, and humility, particularly as a part of God. Zayin embraces the acknowledgment of weakness or failure, avoiding the trap of allowing confidence to become arrogant. It can be considered Divine Humility, the source of giving yourself over to God's will.

ח **Het:** The eighth letter of the Hebrew alphabet. It embodies Yesod, the ninth sephirah on the Tree of Life. This letter is associated with the concepts of foundation, connection, and stability. Het can be called the Foundation or the Link to God, the different realms of existence. There is also an association with congruence and balance across the universe. It is the Divine Connectivity, possessing the building blocks needed for the spiritual and physical components of the world.

ט **Tet:** The ninth letter of the Hebrew alphabet. It is coupled with Malkuth, the tenth and final sephirah on the Tree of Life. This letter epitomizes kingship, sovereignty, and the physical world. Tet, also known as the Kingdom of Queen, is considered the source of physical manifestations within reality. It references God as the ultimate ruler of all things and the highest authority in the universe. The letter Tet expresses the idea of Divine Sovereignty, in which everything in existence falls under the dominion of God.

י **Yod:** The tenth letter of the Hebrew alphabet. It is considered to be the most spiritually powerful and mystical of the letters, maintaining a strong connection to Keter, the first and highest sephirah on the Tree of Life. This letter is linked to both spiritual and divine awareness. Yod can be called the Crown or Will, where God exists as the utmost spiritual reality and the wellspring of resolve and intention. It is considered the Divine Will, expressing all designs and spiritual awareness in the universe.

כ **Kaf:** The eleventh letter of the Hebrew alphabet. It is associated with Chochmah, the second sephirah on the Tree of Life. This letter symbolizes wisdom, intuition, and the origins of creation. Kaf is where creative ideas and intellectual understanding stems, also known as the Wisdom or Supernal Father. The beginning of the universe and spiritual intuition come from here. The letter Kaf represents Divine Wisdom and is considered the place where all worldly wisdom and understanding come from.

ל **Lamed:** The twelfth letter of the Hebrew alphabet. A goad, pastoral staff, shepherd's crook, or cattle prod sometimes represents Lamed. Like Bet, it is associated with Binah and the idea of Divine Understanding. This letter personifies the world's shared empathy, understanding, and comprehension.

מ **Mem:** The thirteenth letter of the Hebrew alphabet. It is coupled with Da'at, the third sephirah on the Tree of Life. This letter contains the characteristics of familiarity, consciousness, and self-awareness. Mem exemplifies spiritual insight, cognizance, and wisdom, referred to as Knowledge or Awareness. Known as Divine Knowledge, it can be considered the source of mindfulness, intellect, and sensibility throughout the universe.

נ **Nun:** The fourteenth letter of the Hebrew alphabet. It is related to Neshamah, one of the five parts of the soul, which consists of morality and emotion. This letter pertains to the attributes of spiritual awareness, divine inspiration, and a deep connection to God. Nun is called the Divine Soul or Spiritual Soul and is associated with Divine Inspiration, considered the source of all spiritual and divine influence worldwide.

ס **Samekh:** The fifteenth letter of the Hebrew alphabet. Like Het, it connects to Yesod, the ninth sephirah on the Tree of Life. This letter embodies the idea of support and infrastructure. It is an expression of the framework of the universe, which exists as part of the foundation of all things. Samekh is also associated with the idea of stability and structure, including the Divine Support that holds up the physical and metaphysical realms.

ע **Ayin:** The sixteenth letter of the Hebrew alphabet. It is associated with Hod, the eighth sephirah on the Tree of Life, just like the letter Zayin. Ayin embodies the traits of humility and gratitude, especially in relation to God's will. It is referred to as subservience or thankfulness, bowing to the majesty and splendor of the Divine Creator. This letter is also connected to Divine Acknowledgment, creating the opening through which you can give yourself over to the designs of the universe.

פ **Pe:** The seventeenth letter of the Hebrew alphabet. Kabbalistic scholarship maintains that the symbol for Pe is based on an open mouth, representing the fact that it follows Ayin, which forms a gateway into the divine by being the apparatus that actually brings the divine into reality. This is usually done through prayer, recitation of the sacred texts, and transfer of divine knowledge. It can be roughly translated as speech, vocalization, or breath and is related to Divine Expression.

צ **Tsadi:** The eighteenth letter of the Hebrew alphabet. It was given its name and symbol due to its resemblance to a fishing hook. This letter can be defined as hunting, capturing, or snaring. The shape of Tsadi can also be viewed as a person bowing in exaltation, conveying that you must humble yourself before the Divine Creator to glory in His works. It represents a righteous person, a faithful servant to God, and the Divine Worshipper.

ק **Qof:** The nineteenth letter of the Hebrew alphabet. It embodies the cyclical nature of the universe and everything therein. This is expressed through the eternal repetition of things like the changing seasons, the life cycles of humans, animals, and plants, as well as the ever-changing and repeating chains of celestial bodies. Just as everything within the natural world experiences birth, growth, decline, death, and rebirth, so too do the planets and stars. Qof also possesses the symbolic action of removing any negative coverings or husks so that the unfettered holiness hidden beneath it can be revealed. It is considered the Divine Wheel, constantly turning over from one aspect of the world to another.

ר **Resh:** The twentieth letter of the Hebrew alphabet. Despite falling near the end of the alphabet, Resh means "beginning" or "head." This letter denotes the idea that "the beginning of wisdom is the fear of God." It is associated with the choice between nobility, decadence, selflessness, and greed. The belief that you should be a leader instead of a follower by emulating the Divine Creator is also connected to Resh.

ש **Shin:** The twenty-first letter of the Hebrew alphabet. It translates to the word "tooth," and its symbol depicts the three pillars of flame. This letter has a strong association with fire, particularly in its function as a purification method. It also represents the fire of God and the divine energy that can cleanse and purify the soul. Shin embodies renewal and balance, with the letter's shape showing the two opposing extremes with the left and right pillars of flame, tempered by the third pillar of flame in the center. It is characterized as Divine Transformation, which sits at the root of all change throughout the universe.

ת **Tav:** The twenty-second and final letter of the Hebrew alphabet. It is defined as a sign, mark, or omen and the symbol of transcendence, fulfillment, and truth. This letter is connected to the concept of restoration, including restoring your spiritual essence to the Divine Creator. The entire universe emanated from God, and the course of its existence leads up to the moment of complete perfection. Since Tav is the last letter in the alphabet, it is followed by a return to the beginning. It is representative of Divine Emanation, containing both the origins and totality of the universe.

Chapter 3: Spheres, Planets, and Stars

The Kabbalistic Tree of Life and its sephirot are associated with astrology through the correlation between the various paths of the Tree of Life and notable celestial bodies. Sephirot and the astrological planets converge to create a complex tapestry of traits, characteristics, symbols, behaviors, spiritual essences, and meanings. Different sephirot match up with certain planets or other celestial bodies, signs of the zodiac, elements, astrological numbers, and Judaic angels and demons. Since it was through the emanations of God that the sephirot, planets, moons, and stars were all created, they possess the mystical and spiritual energies that permeate both the seen and unseen aspects of the universe.

Different planets are matched with sephirot.
Lsmpascal, CC BY-SA 3.0 <https://creativecommons.org/licenses/by-sa/3.0>, via Wikimedia Commons https://commons.wikimedia.org/wiki/File:Size_planets_comparison.jpg

The Astrological Planets

In the context of astrology, astrological planets refer to the planets within our solar system (excluding Earth), as well as the Sun and Moon. Note that while Pluto was downgraded to a "dwarf planet" by the International Astronomical Union (IAU) in 2006, it is still considered a regular planet within astrology. Each astrological planet is associated with specific characteristics and influences that can determine your actions and personality. The placement of the planets in your natal chart is believed to indicate your potential for having certain traits and for experiences to occur in your life. The list of astrological planets and their associations include:

The Sun: Associated with the self, the ego, and one's sense of identity. It is also connected to leadership, ambition, and vitality.

The Moon: Associated with emotions, instincts, and the unconscious mind. It is also connected to the mother, home, and security.

Mercury: Associated with communication, intelligence, and adaptability. It is also connected to travel and transportation.

Venus: Associated with love, beauty, and harmony. It is also connected to money and material possessions.

Mars: Associated with energy, aggression, and determination. It is also connected to sexuality and physical activity.

Jupiter: Associated with expansion, optimism, and good luck. It is also connected to higher education and philosophy.

Saturn: Associated with restriction, discipline, and responsibility. It is also connected to career and long-term goals.

Uranus: Associated with innovation, change, and rebellion. It is also connected to technology and the future.

Neptune: Associated with mysticism, illusion, and spirituality. It is also connected to art and imagination.

Pluto: Associated with transformation, power, and regeneration. It is also connected to sex and death.

The Sephirot and the Astrological Planets

The sephirot are all ruled by certain astrological planets possessing shared aspects and characteristics between them. Each planet (excluding Earth), the Sun, the Moon, and the four elements can be connected with a sephirah, notable symbol, defining trait, astrological number, color, flower, gemstone, angel, demon, and sign of the zodiac. The specific meaning of these characteristics helps to flesh out the connections made by the sephirot in the Tree of Life. It can all be taken as pieces of a larger puzzle, and you can observe the links by understanding the following:

The Sun

Sephirah: Tiferet
Symbol: Butterfly
Trait: Beauty
Number: 1
Color: Yellow
Flower: Sunflower
Gemstone: Ruby
Angel: Michael
Demon: Mammon
Zodiac Sign: Aries

The Moon

Sephirah: Yesod
Symbol: Crescent
Trait: Foundation
Number: 2
Colors: White and Silver
Flower: Moonflower
Gemstones: Pearl or Moonstone
Angel: Gabriel
Demon: Belphegor
Zodiac Sign: Cancer

Mercury

Sephirah: Hod
Symbol: Coin
Trait: Splendor
Number: 5
Colors: Blue and Yellow
Flower: Lavender
Gemstone: Emerald
Angel: Raphael
Demon: Beelzebub
Zodiac Sign: Gemini

Venus

Sephirah: Netsach
Symbol: Ouroboros
Trait: Victory
Number: 6
Color: Green
Flower: Rose
Gemstone: Diamond
Angel: Haniel
Demon: Lucifer
Zodiac Sign: Taurus

Mars

Sephirah: Geburah
Symbol: Lion
Trait: Courage
Number: 9
Color: Red
Flower: Peruvian Lily
Gemstone: Bloodstone

Angel: Samael
Demon: Lilith
Zodiac Sign: Leo

Jupiter

Sephirah: Chesed
Symbol: Heart
Trait: Mercy
Number: 3
Color: Purple
Flower: Carnation
Gemstone: Yellow Sapphire
Angel: Zadkiel
Demon: Hismael
Zodiac Sign: Sagittarius

Saturn

Sephirah: Binah
Symbol: Scythe
Trait: Understanding
Number: 8
Color: Brown
Flower: Amaranth
Gemstone: Iolite
Angel: Cassiel
Demon: Zazel
Zodiac Sign: Capricorn

Uranus

Sephirah: Keter
Symbol: Crown
Trait: Willpower
Number: 4

Color: Pink
Flower: Primrose
Gemstone: Rose Quartz
Angel: Uriel
Demon: Asmodeus
Zodiac Sign: Libra

Neptune

Sephirah: Chochmah
Symbol: Trident
Trait: Wisdom
Number: 7
Color: Sea Blue
Flower: Water Lily
Gemstone: Topaz
Angel: Raziel
Demon: Barbas
Zodiac Signs: Pisces and Aquarius

Pluto

Sephirah: Da'at
Symbol: Owl
Trait: Knowledge
Number: 10
Color: Black
Flower: Narcissus
Gemstone: Onyx
Angel: Azrael
Demon: Hecate
Zodiac Sign: Scorpio

The Four Elements

Sephirah: Malkuth
Symbols: Earth, Air, Fire, Water
Trait: Sovereignty
Number: 0
Colors: Brown
Flower: Daisy
Gemstones: Agate (Earth), Amethyst (Air), Citrine (Fire), Opal (Water)
Angel: Zuriel
Demon: Leviathan
Zodiac Sign: Virgo

Chapter 4: Through the Zodiac I. Cardinal Signs

In astrology, the zodiac is divided into 12 signs, each associated with one of the four cardinal directions: north, south, east, and west. The "cardinal signs" are the four signs that fall at the beginning of each season: Aries, Cancer, Libra, and Capricorn. They are considered the frontrunners to the rest of the zodiac and share a number of characteristics with one another. This includes assigning a specific element to each cardinal sign and a particularly significant day during its associated season. The elements are the four classical elements, corresponding to the four cardinal signs, and they connect to either solstices or equinoxes.

    The cardinal signs also have an important role in Kabbalah. The energy of the sephirot on the Tree of Life is rooted in its connection to the zodiac, where the position and direction of celestial bodies and phenomena help inform the sephirot's influences. Depending on which ones are coupled with your own natal chart, the type of person you are, your attributes, and your path can all be traced back to both the sephirot and the zodiac. Anyone can benefit from learning more about themselves, especially if they have questions about aspects of their own life. It's another avenue for self-reflection and self-improvement that is necessary for you to continue growing.

Characteristics of the Zodiac Signs

Those connected to the cardinal signs are known to be strong leaders, often taking the initiative with things in their life. They are usually proactive, ready to step up and take charge of situations at any moment. People born under the cardinal signs are also ambitious, seeking to take a strategic approach when it comes to achieving their goals. They can be viewed as the "corners" of the zodiac, marking the beginning of a new season and a new growth cycle.

The Golden Dawn

The Hermetic Order of the Golden Dawn was a secret society primarily active around the late 19th and early 20th centuries. They were well-known for practicing ceremonial magic and delving into the occult and were originally founded using the teachings of Kabbalah and the Rosicrucians, an esoteric Christian fraternity that was part of a larger cultural movement in Europe involving spiritualism during the 17th century. The Golden Dawn was heavily influenced by the work of Eliphas Levi, an infamous British occultist, and the ceremonial magic used by the Hermetic Order of the Asiatic Brethren.

The Rose Cross represents the Golden Dawn.
Dm, CC0, via Wikimedia Commons https://commons.wikimedia.org/wiki/File:Taro_Rose_Cross.svg

The Golden Dawn was founded in London in 1888 by Dr. William Robert Woodman, William Wynn Westcott, and Samuel Liddell MacGregor Mathers. All three were members of the Freemasons, and Freemasonry had a major impact on the Golden Dawn, especially in how it was set up with smaller, decentralized lodges, a hierarchy with increasing degrees to denote prominence, and secret, ritualistic initiation rites. However, unlike the Freemasons, they allowed women to become members and advance through the ranks on an equal footing with the men.

The Golden Dawn became one of the most influential occult organizations of its time, attracting many prominent members of the day. Some of their more notable recruits included the acclaimed Irish poet, writer, and dramatist William Butler Yeats, British author and Sherlock Holmes scribe Sir Arthur Conan Doyle, and the divisive English writer and occultist Aleister Crowley, who would later go on to find his own esoteric religion known as Thelema. Highly respected members of society, such as artists, writers, philosophers, and doctors, could be found among their ranks. During the Age of Enlightenment, when intellectualism, reason, and the push for empirical evidence spread throughout Europe, the Golden Dawn was an attractive alternative to traditional religions.

The organization had a hierarchical structure where members were initiated into various grades, each possessing its own set of teachings, rituals, and practices. There were three Orders that members could advance through, and each Order was broken down into grades with paired numbers. The paired numbers within each Order were related to positions on the Tree of Life. The Golden Dawn imparted knowledge on subjects like magic, alchemy, astrology, Tarot, and Kabbalah. It also focused on the development of psychic abilities, clairvoyance, and astral projection.

Despite the influential members within the Golden Dawn, it was officially dissolved as an organization in 1903. However, its teachings and practices still went on to have a significant impact on modern occultism and esotericism, even seeing some of them adopted by the very same traditions that inspired it. Many of its members also went on to form their own mystical and occult-centric organizations, carrying what they learned from the Golden Dawn into their new ventures. Contemporary esoteric groups, such as the Hermetic Brotherhood of Luxor, can trace their roots directly back to the Golden Dawn.

The Tetragrammaton

The Tetragrammaton is the four-letter name of the Hebrew God – YHWH – and it is considered the most sacred and holy name in all of Judaism. It is often referred to as the "ineffable name" or "unutterable name," as the Jewish people believed it was so holy that it should never be spoken out loud. Instead, the Hebrew word "Adonai," which means "Lord," is typically substituted for it when reading from the Hebrew Bible (also known in Christianity as the Old Testament). The exact pronunciation of the Tetragrammaton is "Jehovah" or "Yahweh." Although the name appears 6,828 times in the Hebrew Bible, the precise pronunciation has been lost to time, so nobody is certain how to say it correctly.

The Tetragrammaton.
https://openclipart.org/detail/307583/esoteric-staff-remix

In the context of Kabbalah, the Tetragrammaton is associated with the sephirah of Keter, the highest of the ten emanations of God and through which He created the entire universe. It also has a connection with the four elements, the four cardinal directions, and the four worlds of creation. The Tetragrammaton is central to the practice of theurgic magic, which uses special rituals and meditations to invoke the presence of God.

As with Judaism, the Tetragrammaton in Christianity is seen as the original name of God. Jesus is considered the embodiment of the name, being sent to Earth by God to execute His will in the form of a mortal man. The Tetragrammaton is not used in Islam, but Allah, their name for God, is viewed as sacred and sits above all other names for Him. Because the Tetragrammaton is considered a very sacred and holy name in Judaism, there are strict religious rules and customs regarding its use and pronunciation. Even writing the word "God" is regarded as taboo, so many sections of Jewish culture will instead replace the "o" in God with a dash, rendering it as "G-d."

Characteristics of the Cardinal Signs

In addition to the traditional Kabbalistic version of cardinal signs, both the Golden Dawn and the Tetragrammaton have traits and characteristics intrinsically linked to them. The primary attributes associated with the four cardinal signs include:

Aries

Aries is the first sign of the zodiac and the first cardinal sign. It marks the beginning of the astrological year and is associated with the energy of initiation, leadership, and action. Those born under Aries are said to be ambitious and confident, always eager to take on new challenges and explore new horizons.

Zodiac Symbol: The Ram
Cardinal Direction: East
Seasonal Day: Vernal Equinox (start of spring)
Sephirah: Geburah
Kabbalistic Path: Netsach to Yesod
Ruling Planet: Mars
Element: Fire
Key Concept: Initiative
Energy Type: Masculine
Hebrew Month: Nisan
Hebrew Letters: He and Dalet
Tetragrammaton Letters: He-Vav-He-Yod (יהוה)
Guiding Angel: Malahidael

Major Arcana Tarot Card: The Emperor
Minor Arcana Tarot Cards: 2, 3, 4 of Wands
Number: 44
Color: Red
Day: Tuesday
Wood: Dogwood
Metal: Steel or Iron
Flower: Geranium, Sweetpea, or Daisy
Herb: Thistle
Essential Oils: Frankincense, Pine, and Neroli
Gemstone: Diamond
Power Stone: Ruby

Cancer

Cancer is the fourth sign of the zodiac and the second cardinal sign. It is associated with the energy of nurturing, emotional intelligence, and family. Those born with Cancer are said to be deeply sensitive, intuitive, and protective of those about whom they care.

Zodiac Symbol: The Crab
Cardinal Direction: North
Seasonal Day: Summer Solstice (start of summer)
Sephirah: Yesod
Kabbalistic Path: Binah to Geburah
Ruling Planet: The Moon
Element: Water
Key Concept: Receptivity
Energy Type: Feminine
Hebrew Month: Tammuz
Hebrew Letters: Tav-Het
Tetragrammaton Letters: He-Vav-He-Yod (יהוה)
Guiding Angel: Muriel
Major Arcana Tarot Card: The Chariot
Minor Arcana Tarot Cards: 2, 3, 4 of Cups

Number: 69
Color: Yellow-Orange
Day: Monday
Wood: Holly
Metal: Silver
Flower: Jasmine or Gardenia
Herb: Honeysuckle
Essential Oils: Myrrh and Chamomile
Gemstone: Chriscola
Power Stones: Moonstone and Emerald

Libra

Libra is the seventh sign of the zodiac and the third cardinal sign. It is associated with the energy of balance, harmony, and diplomacy. Those born under Libra are said to be charming, cooperative, and tactful, able to bring people together and mediate conflicts.

Zodiac Symbol: The Scales
Cardinal Direction: West
Seasonal Day: Autumnal Equinox (start of autumn)
Sephirah: Netsach
Kabbalistic Path: Tiferet to Geburah
Ruling Planet: Venus
Element: Air
Key Concept: Harmony
Energy Type: Masculine
Hebrew Month: Tishrei
Hebrew Letters: Lamed-Pe
Tetragrammaton Letters: Vav-He-Yod-He (והיה)
Guiding Angel: Zuriel
Major Arcana Tarot Card: Justice
Minor Arcana Tarot Cards: 2, 3, 4 of Swords
Number: 33
Color: Green

Day: Friday
Wood: Poplar
Metal: Copper
Flower: Rose
Herb: Thyme
Essential Oils: Sandalwood, Rose, and Clary
Gemstone: Opal
Power Stone: Diamond

Capricorn

Capricorn is the tenth sign of the zodiac and the fourth cardinal sign. It is associated with the energy of structure, responsibility, and ambition. Those born under Capricorn are said to be disciplined, hardworking, and goal-oriented, capable of setting and achieving objectives through determination and focus.

Zodiac Symbol: The Goat
Cardinal Direction: South
Seasonal Day: Winter Solstice (start of winter)
Sephirah: Binah
Kabbalistic Path: Hod to Tiferet
Ruling Planet: Saturn
Element: Earth
Key Concept: Structure
Energy Type: Feminine
Hebrew Month: Tevet
Hebrew Letters: Bet-Ayin
Tetragrammaton Letters: He-Yod-He-Vav (היהו)
Guiding Angel: Hanael
Major Arcana Tarot Card: The Devil
Minor Arcana Tarot Cards: 2, 3, 4 of Pentacles
Number: 23
Color: Blue-Violet
Day: Saturday

Wood: Birch
Metal: Lead
Flower: Carnation
Herb: Comfrey Root
Essential Oils: Juniper, Chamomile, Cedarwood, Spearmint, and Fennel
Gemstone: Onyx
Power Stone: Quartz Crystal

Chapter 5: Through the Zodiac II. Fixed Signs

The fixed signs of the zodiac are Taurus, Leo, Scorpio, and Aquarius. These signs are known for their determination and stability. They are considered "fixed" because they possess a fixed modality characterized by persistence, determination, and a strong sense of purpose. Fixed signs can be considered the stabilizers of the zodiac, taking the enthusiastic, creative ideas of the cardinal signs and turning them into something concrete and realistically applicable.

Characteristics of the Fixed Signs

As with the cardinal signs, the traditional Kabbalistic version of fixed signs also has traits and characteristics connected to the Golden Dawn and the Tetragrammaton. The primary attributes associated with the four fixed signs include:

Taurus

Taurus is the second sign of the zodiac and the first fixed sign. It is associated with the material world, including money, possessions, and physical pleasure. Those born under Taurus are said to be loyal, reliable, stubborn, and realistic in matters of the world.

Zodiac Symbol: The Bull
Seasonal Day: May Day (middle of spring)
Sephirah: Nesach
Kabbalistic Path: Chochmah to Chesed
Ruling Planet: Venus
Element: Earth
Key Concept: Stability
Energy Type: Feminine
Hebrew Month: Iyar
Hebrew Letters: Vav-Pe
Tetragrammaton Letters: Yod-He-He-Vav (יההו)
Guiding Angel: Asmodel
Major Arcana Tarot Card: The Hierophant
Minor Arcana Tarot Cards: 5, 6, 7 of Pentacles
Number: 42
Color: Red-Orange
Day: Friday
Wood: Willow
Metal: Copper
Flower: Narcissus
Herb: Sage
Essential Oils: Rose, Patchouli, and Lilac
Gemstone: Emerald
Power Stone: Agate

Leo

Leo is the fifth sign of the zodiac and the second fixed sign. It is associated with strength, creativity, self-expression, and leadership. Those born under Leo are said to be passionate, theatrical, protective, and generous.

Zodiac Symbol: The Lion
Seasonal Day: Midsummer (middle of summer)
Sephirah: Tiferet

Kabbalistic Path: Geburah to Chesed
Ruling Planet: The Sun
Element: Fire
Key Concept: Magnetism
Energy Type: Masculine
Hebrew Month: Av
Hebrew Letters: Tet-Kaf
Tetragrammaton Letters: He-Vav-Yod-He (הויה)
Guiding Angel: Verchiel
Major Arcana Tarot Card: Strength
Minor Arcana Tarot Cards: 5, 6, 7 of Wands
Number: 9
Color: Yellow
Day: Sunday
Wood: Hazel
Metal: Gold
Flower: Sunflower or Marigold
Herb: St. John's Wort
Essential Oils: Cinnamon, Cedar, and Orange
Gemstone: Ruby
Power Stone: Amber

Scorpio

Scorpio is the eighth sign of the zodiac and the third fixed sign. It is associated with intensity, depth, and transformation. Those born under Scorpio are said to be honest, ambitious, temperamental, and have a strategic mind.

Zodiac Symbol: The Scorpion
Seasonal Day: Sukkot (middle of autumn)
Sephirah: Da'at
Kabbalistic Path: Tiferet to Netsach
Ruling Planet: Pluto
Element: Water

Key Concept: Intensity
Energy Type: Feminine
Hebrew Month: Cheshvan
Hebrew Letters: Nun-Dalet
Tetragrammaton Letters: Vav-He-He-Yod (וההי)
Guiding Angel: Barbiel
Major Arcana Tarot Card: Death
Minor Arcana Tarot Cards: 5, 6, 7 of Cups
Number: 72
Color: Blue-Green
Day: Tuesday
Wood: Hemlock
Metal: Iron
Flower: Chrysanthemum
Herb: Wormwood
Essential Oils: Tuberose and Rosemary
Gemstone: Topaz
Power Stone: Garnet

Aquarius

Aquarius is the eleventh sign of the zodiac and the fourth fixed sign. It is associated with innovation, progress, and social change. Those born under Aquarius are said to be practical, forward-thinking, humanitarian, and capable of ingenious solutions to problems.

Zodiac Symbol: The Water Bearer
Seasonal Day: Midwinter (middle of winter)
Sephirah: Binah
Kabbalistic Path: Chochmah to Tiferet
Ruling Planet: Saturn
Element: Air
Key Concept: Eccentricity
Energy Type: Masculine
Hebrew Month: Shevat

Hebrew Letters: Bet-Tsadi
Tetragrammaton Letters: He-Yod-Vav-He (היוה)
Guiding Angel: Cambiel
Major Arcana Tarot Card: The Star
Minor Arcana Tarot Cards: 5, 6, 7 of Swords
Number: 51
Color: Violet
Day: Saturday
Wood: Ash
Metal: Aluminum
Flower: Orchid
Herb: Valerian
Essential Oils: Fennel Oil and Lemon Verbena
Gemstone: Amethyst
Power Stone: Sapphire

Chapter 6: Through the Zodiac III. Mutable Signs

The mutable signs of the zodiac are Gemini, Virgo, Sagittarius, and Pisces. They are considered flexible and adaptable, more capable of evolving than the other signs. Mutable signs come at the end of each season, presaging the transformation from one to another. These signs thrive on change but also have a restless nature, never wanting to stay in one place or do one thing for a long time. The mutable signs can take the ideas solidified by the fixed signs and whittle down the rougher edges, perfecting them.

Characteristics of the Mutable Signs

Like with the cardinal and fixed signs, the traditional Kabbalistic version of mutable signs also have traits and characteristics connected to the Golden Dawn and the Tetragrammaton. The primary attributes associated with the four mutable signs include:

Gemini

Gemini is the third sign of the zodiac and the first mutable sign. It is associated with communication, information, and duality. Those born under Gemini are said to be cunning, perceptive, adaptable, contrarian, and can easily navigate most social situations.

Zodiac Symbol: The Twins
Seasonal Transition: End of spring to start of summer
Sephirah: Hod
Kabbalistic Path: Binah to Tiferet
Ruling Planet: Mercury
Element: Air
Key Concept: Variety
Energy Type: Masculine
Hebrew Month: Sivan
Hebrew Letters: Zayin-Resh
Tetragrammaton Letters: Yod-Vav-He-He (יוהה)
Guiding Angel: Ambriel
Major Arcana Tarot Card: The Lovers
Minor Arcana Tarot Cards: 8, 9, 10 of Swords
Number: 14
Color: Orange
Day: Wednesday
Wood: Oak
Metal: Mercury
Flower: Violets
Herb: Parsley
Essential Oils: Lavender, Lemongrass, and Benzoin
Gemstone: Agate
Power Stone: Aquamarine

Virgo

Virgo is the sixth sign of the zodiac and the second mutable sign. It is associated with order, intelligence, discernment, and craftsmanship. Those born under Virgo are said to be detail-oriented, have plenty of common sense, and often take up career paths where they perform service, such as in the military, clerical jobs, government positions, and manual labor.

Zodiac Symbol: The Virgin
Seasonal Transition: End of summer to start of autumn
Sephirah: Hod
Kabbalistic Path: Tiferet to Chesed
Ruling Planet: Mercury
Element: Earth
Key Concept: Perfection
Energy Type: Feminine
Hebrew Month: Elul
Hebrew Letters: Yod-Resh
Tetragrammaton Letters: He-He-Vav-Yod (ההוי)
Guiding Angel: Hamaliel
Major Arcana Tarot Card: The Hermit
Minor Arcana Tarot Cards: 8, 9, 10 of Pentacles
Number: 5
Color: Yellow-Green
Day: Wednesday
Wood: Aspen
Metal: Pewter
Flower: Morning Glory
Herb: Dill
Essential Oils: Lemon Balm, Caraway, and Sage
Gemstone: Peridot
Power Stone: Amethyst

Sagittarius

Sagittarius is the ninth sign of the zodiac and the third mutable sign. It is associated with philosophy, exploration, abstract intelligence, and higher education. Those born under Sagittarius are said to be adventurous, optimistic, and clever – and have a deep appreciation for nature.

Zodiac Symbol: The Archer
Seasonal Transition: End of autumn to start of winter
Sephirah: Chesed

Kabbalistic Path: Tiferet to Geburah
Ruling Planet: Jupiter
Element: Fire
Key Concept: Expansion
Energy Type: Masculine
Hebrew Month: Kislev
Hebrew Letters: Gimel-Samekh
Tetragrammaton Letters: Vav-Yod-He-He (ויהה)
Guiding Angel: Advachiel
Major Arcana Tarot Card: Temperance
Minor Arcana Tarot Cards: 8, 9, 10 of Wands
Number: 65
Color: Blue
Day: Thursday
Wood: Elder
Metal: Tin
Flower: Iris
Herb: Chicory
Essential Oils: Clove, Juniper Berry, and Vetiver
Gemstone: Turquoise
Power Stone: Lapis Lazuli

Pisces

Pisces is the twelfth sign of the zodiac and the fourth mutable sign. It is associated with imagination, compassion, spirituality, and unconditional love. Those born under Pisces are said to be artistic, empathetic, naïve, and possess a sense of idealism.

Zodiac Symbol: The Fish
Seasonal Transition: End of winter to start of spring
Sephirah: Chochmah
Kabbalistic Path: Netsach to Malkuth
Ruling Planet: Neptune
Element: Water

Key Concept: Compassion
Energy Type: Feminine
Hebrew Month: Adar
Hebrew Letters: Gimel-Qof
Tetragrammaton Letters: He-He-Yod-Vav (ההיו)
Guiding Angel: Barchiel
Major Arcana Tarot Card: The Moon
Minor Arcana Tarot Cards: 8, 9, 10 of Cups
Number: 34
Color: Violet-Red
Day: Thursday
Wood: Wild Olive
Metal: Platinum
Flower: Hyacinth
Herb: Yarrow
Essential Oils: Gardenia, Camphor, and Jasmine
Gemstone: Aquamarine
Power Stone: Tourmaline

Chapter 7: Lessons of the Lunar Nodes

The lunar nodes play an important role in Kabbalistic astrology. This stems from their astronomical significance, as whenever a full moon is close enough to one of the lunar nodes, there will be a lunar eclipse, and when a new moon is near them, a solar eclipse will occur. They can also influence the ocean's tides, causing them to become lower than usual. However, due to global warming and the rising sea level, the precession of lunar nodes will likely contribute to an increase in coastal flooding by the 2030s.

The Lunar Nodes

Lunar nodes are the two points in space where the moon's orbit intersects the plane of Earth's orbit around the sun, also known as the ecliptic plane. The point where the moon moves north of the ecliptic plane is called the ascending node, and the point where it moves south of the ecliptic plane is called the descending node. In astrology, the lunar nodes are considered important points in your natal chart and are often used to interpret these charts.

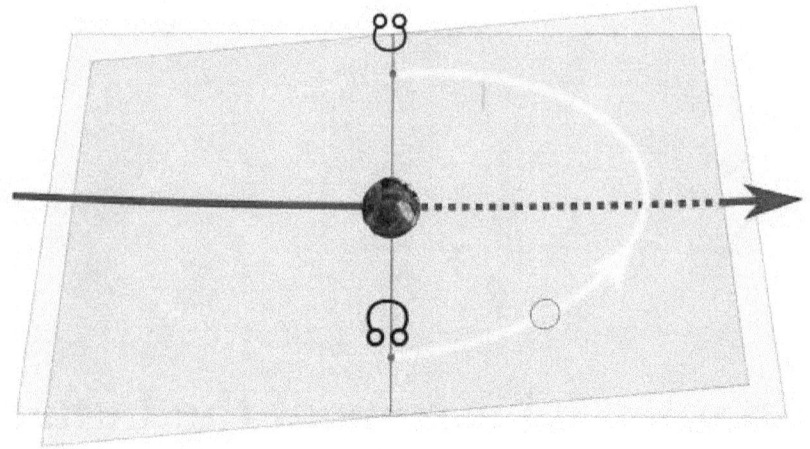

The north and south lunar nodes.
Episcophagus, CC BY-SA 4.0 <https://creativecommons.org/licenses/by-sa/4.0>, via Wikimedia Commons https://commons.wikimedia.org/wiki/File:Lunar_nodes.svg

Lunar Precession

Lunar precession is the gradual change in the orientation of the moon's rotational axis in space. It is caused by the gravitational pull of the sun and the Earth on the moon's equatorial bulge, causing the moon's axis to move in a small circle. This movement, called precession, impacts the moon's poles by pointing them in slightly different directions over time. The precession of the moon's rotational axis will result in an alteration to the moon's apparent position in the sky, which is something that can be observed over a period of 18.6 years. This is known as the lunar nodal cycle. The precession of the moon also affects the position of the lunar nodes since they are determined by the location where the orbit of the moon crosses the ecliptic.

The North (Ascending) Node

The north or ascending node is the point in the orbit of the moon where it moves from the southern hemisphere of the sky to the northern hemisphere, as viewed from the Earth. It represents the types of experiences you need to cultivate to improve your karma and evolve spiritually. In Kabbalistic astrology, the north node is also called the *tikkun*. It is considered the karmic adjustment your soul needs to carry out before it can grow. Your tikkun aids your personal development and brings forth new opportunities. It symbolizes the beginning of your journey when you are still inexperienced and have plenty of progress yet to be made.

The South (Descending) Node

The south or descending node is the point in the moon's orbit where it crosses over from the northern hemisphere of the sky to the southern hemisphere from the vantage point of Earth. It represents the traits and experiences that come naturally to you. However, they may be overdeveloped and serve as a crutch that you fall back on since they tend to be within your comfort zone. In Kabbalistic astrology, the south node is considered a point of release, where you must let go of old habits, attachments, and behaviors. It is associated with karmic patterns and symbolizes the people, places, things, and events you need to part from to develop as an individual.

Kabbalah and the Lunar Nodes

Regarding Kabbalistic astrology, the lunar nodes can help you answer important questions about your destiny, karmic path, and identities in past lives. You can find out why you exist, what you're meant to do with your life, and where you should focus your energy. The different combinations of north and south nodes will create a unique set of characteristics, destinies, and incarnations that you can use to help guide you when determining your future.

Combinations of the North and South Nodes

Although the north and south nodes are completely opposite from one another, they can work together when combined to establish a specific group of characteristics that will move to the forefront. These combinations include:

North Node in Aries and South Node in Libra

Life: You need to learn how to become more self-reliant, as you have a tendency to place all of your focus on your current relationships. Don't let your partnerships define you; you have plenty of great attributes as an individual. Move on from any toxic situations you're involved in, as it isn't worth the harm it does to your being. While relationships require a lot of work, you have to be secure with yourself before you can put in the effort necessary to sustain them.

Destiny: You are on a journey of self-discovery and will be a pioneer with your ideas.

Incarnation: In a past life, you were driven and self-sufficient. You were likely an ambitious and successful person in your professional life, but your relationships might have suffered because of it. Use your current life to work on improving your relationships with others, but don't allow them to consume you.

North Node in Taurus and South Node in Scorpio

Life: You enjoy the finer things in life, but you can also be too generous and hedonistic. You're likely in charge of your family's finances rather than your partner. Maintaining consistency in the flow of your emotions and keeping promises is essential since you tend to be too focused on personal evolution. Don't put up too many walls; it's okay to let others in, especially someone as trusted as a romantic partner.

Destiny: You are on a journey of experiencing a sharing of resources with a spouse or partner and building your wealth on your own terms.

Incarnation: In a past life, you were fiercely independent, never relying on anyone else to help you out with anything. However, you may have become too greedy, losing sight of what's truly important. Use your current life to balance your personal and professional lives, finding a comfortable medium between both aspects of your existence.

North Node in Gemini and South Node in Sagittarius

Life: You are an independent thinker and possess great communication skills. Whether it's through speaking or writing, you say what you mean and rely on facts to get your point across. Seeing new places and meeting new people is your favorite activity, and you enjoy a challenge. After all your diverse experiences, you will return enriched and ready to pass on all that you've learned to others.

Destiny: You are on a journey of discovering new and exciting things worldwide and using your own experiences to communicate the lessons learned to those in an earlier phase of their lives.

Incarnation: In a past life, you were an explorer or adventurer and often spoke about your experiences as a great orator or author. Use your current life to learn about the world and share these ideas without forgetting to return home.

North Node in Cancer and South Node in Capricorn

Life: You constantly struggle between your professional career and your growing family. Sometimes, you can be too ambitious, forgetting to cultivate relationships with people outside of work. Focusing on your job is a way to cope with problems in your life, leading you to neglect the other facets of your world. Make sure to also take care of your needs, giving yourself time to rest and recuperate.

Destiny: You are journeying to nurture your private and professional lives so they can both be fulfilling. In a tug-of-war between the two, it's likely that the family side will come out on top.

Incarnation: In a past life, you were overly invested in your career, and your romantic and familial relationships suffered for it. Use your current life to learn how to be emotionally sensitive to the needs of others. This can take your relationships to a new level.

North Node in Leo and South Node in Aquarius

Life: Artistic and creative endeavors are your bread and butter. You tend to be a dreamer, and while this doesn't always result in realistic goals, reaching for the stars can sometimes work out for you. While you prefer to be part of a group or team, you rarely take on a leadership role. You long to be noticed, but you're uncomfortable in the spotlight. However, once you've seen how people respond to your talents, it will become easier to step outside your comfort zone and shine.

Destiny: You are on a journey of creative expression, seeking to make a name for yourself in the world of arts and entertainment. It's a difficult road to walk, but if you stick with it and believe in yourself, you might just go the distance.

Incarnation: In a past life, you were brimming with creativity but hesitant to take a chance. You played it safe and stuck with an unglamorous career as a safety net. Use your current life to learn how to take the reins, which can elevate you to new heights.

North Node in Virgo and South Node in Pisces

Life: You are a nurturer, always looking to heal the hurts of others. However, you must first heal yourself before you can be as effective as possible. Some of your ideas are a bit too extreme and are unlikely to ever move from the realms of fantasy into reality. This doesn't mean giving up on your dreams – it just means you must manage your expectations. Keeping up with a routine and establishing positive daily habits can help you overcome your tendency to let things in the present slip by you while thinking about the future.

Destiny: You are on a journey of transformation. Look for opportunities to improve yourself, but never ignore your drive to help others in their own personal development.

Incarnation: In a past life, you were someone with many health issues. This has made you very empathetic to those in a similar situation, and you are sensitive to their physical and emotional needs. Use your current life to become more critical and assertive. Don't let people push you around because you show sympathy for others. While you have a tendency to disappear into the spiritual world, ignoring your own relationships, you have a chance to become more communicative.

North Node in Libra and South Node in Aries

Life: You are naturally independent, but you also tend to speak or act impulsively. Learning to work cooperatively and love others freely will be challenging, as you're used to putting your needs first. Now, you have to focus on others.

Destiny: You are on a journey of learning lessons about commitment in your relationships and partnerships. While you are a leader and self-reliant, you don't need to do everything by yourself.

Incarnation: In a past life, you were a lone wolf, working hard to ensure you never needed anyone else's help to survive. However, this cuts you off from the benefits of maintaining close relationships. Use your current life to learn how to be more diplomatic with others, showing a willingness to listen to their ideas instead of always forging ahead with your own.

North Node in Scorpio and South Node in Taurus

Life: You have a deep connection to the spiritual and metaphysical worlds. Because of this, you tend to rely on the support of others to help you survive, especially financially. Whether through receiving an inheritance or marrying a wealthy spouse, you have the freedom to focus your energy on things beyond putting food on the table and a roof over your head. You can sometimes become too obsessed with your current endeavors, and addiction is a very real danger for you.

Destiny: You are on a journey of spiritual enrichment, experiencing the mystical side of the world that most people ignore.

Incarnation: In a past life, you were a trust fund baby or stay-at-home spouse. Use your current life to improve your ability to manage your own affairs, and be patient when it comes to finding your path. Don't hesitate to trust your intuition. Let it help you navigate the treacherous waters and get you to a place where you don't feel controlled or trapped.

North Node in Sagittarius and South Node in Gemini

Life: You are a very talkative person, but you can sometimes lack focus. There is a constant drive within you to seek out wisdom from many different places, and you enjoy learning new things. However, you also tend to change from one subject to another the moment you start to become bored. You are easily distracted, yet when you can put your mind to it, you can find great success.

Destiny: You are on a journey of applying the wealth of knowledge you've accrued to practical purposes. Your generosity with others will come through both with resources and information.

Incarnation: In a past life, you were a teacher or philosopher. However, you remained stuck in the world of academia. Use your current life to take everything you've learned and try them out in the real world. Don't just talk about something – get out there and actually do it.

North Node in Capricorn and South Node in Cancer

Life: You are very pragmatic, seeking opportunities with the best chance of success. Your hard work and motivation stem from a need for approval, which you get quite frequently. In certain aspects of your life, you're an idealist and humanitarian, but you can also be a bit selfish and needy at times. Although you are very goal-oriented and strive to be the best at your chosen profession, you do not want to seek fame.

Destiny: You are pursuing personal fulfillment and finding a healthy work-life balance while pursuing your goals.

Incarnation: In a past life, you were a successful behind-the-scenes person. However, your ambitions were somewhat limited by your tendency to avoid taking too many risks. Use your current life to branch out and set some goals which may seem out of reach. You might just surprise yourself with your ability to achieve them, despite the smaller chance of success.

North Node in Aquarius and South Node in Leo

Life: You are the kind of person whose biggest desire is to leave the world a better place than you found it. When it comes to things like politics and governments, you usually take a more liberal or progressive stance. However, you also enjoy being the center of attention, and some of your efforts can come off as self-aggrandizing rather than humanitarian. Continue to develop as a person, and these issues will disappear in time.

Destiny: You are on a journey of social justice, giving a voice to the people who are too often forgotten by the rest of the world.

Incarnation: In a past life, you were a social activist, focusing a great deal on helping others and fighting for a cause. Use your current life to temper some of your more aggressive personality traits so you can learn how to negotiate and compromise in order to benefit everyone.

North Node in Pisces and South Node in Virgo

Life: You are someone that focuses on the big picture, undertaking endeavors that will initiate change for huge swathes of people. You can sometimes lack boundaries, as you're always pushing others to improve. Since you're a perfectionist, you expect that same level of commitment from the people around you.

Destiny: You are on a journey to change the world through visionary ideas or innovative actions.

Incarnation: In a past life, you were a scientist, doctor, or inventor on the cutting edge of science and technology. You constantly sought to improve on what came before, no matter how complacent others in your field might have become. Use your current life to relax a bit. While you can still push the envelope, take some time to find a calming hobby that doesn't require you to always be driving forward and putting in 110% effort.

Chapter 8: Reading the Kabbalistic Natal Chart

Now that you're better acquainted with the planets and zodiac signs, it's time to put all of that knowledge to good use and learn how to interpret a Kabbalistic natal chart. The stars, planets, and other celestial bodies can significantly affect you as a person, even if you don't realize it. Becoming more familiar with each aspect of a natal chart will make it easier to determine the best way to interpret the signs and other information it can provide.

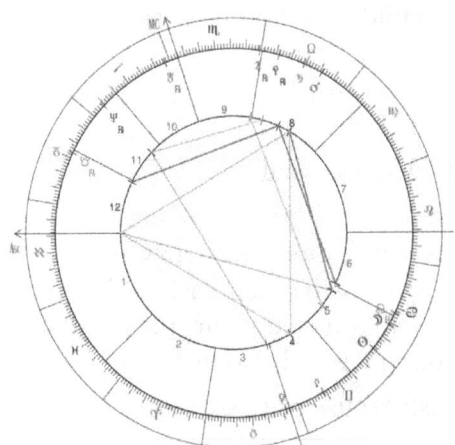

An example of a natal chart.
Morn, CC BY-SA 3.0 <https://creativecommons.org/licenses/by-sa/3.0>, via Wikimedia Commons https://commons.wikimedia.org/wiki/File:Natal_Chart_--_Adam.svg

What Is the Kabbalistic Natal Chart?

The Kabbalistic Natal Chart is a chart used in Kabbalistic astrology to understand the spiritual aspects of your life, including your soul's purpose, strengths, and challenges. It is believed that the chart can reveal the potential of your spiritual path and explain how you can best fulfill your purpose in life. The natal chart is created by analyzing the positions of the planets and other celestial bodies at the time of your birth and then interpreting them according to Kabbalistic principles.

The Astrological Houses

In astrology, the horoscope chart is divided into 12 astrological houses. These houses represent different areas of life and are determined by the time and location of a person's birth. Each house corresponds to a different zodiac sign and planet, and these astrological symbols provide insight into various aspects of someone's life, such as their career, relationships, family, and health. Each house also has a natural ruling planet, which is the planet that governs the affairs of the house and is considered to be the strongest planet in that house.

The 12 houses are usually depicted on a wheel, with the 1st house set around 9:00 and each subsequent house found by moving counter-clockwise. The 1st through 6th houses are the personal houses. They govern a person's private life; those born under these may have trouble moving on from their childhood home or friends. The 7th through 12th houses are the interpersonal houses. They rule a person's relationships; those born under these may tend to leave the past behind. These houses and their descriptions include:

1st House (Aries): House of Self

The 1st House, also called the Ascendant or Rising Sign, represents the self, personality, physical appearance, first impressions, and a general outlook on life. It is ruled by the planet Mars. Celestial bodies transiting into this house will let you see your ideas, viewpoints, and other endeavors solidify. Your goals will also finally be made manifest.

2nd House (Taurus): House of Possessions

The 2nd House represents material possessions, personal finances, daily routines, work ethic, and self-worth. It is ruled by the planet Venus. When celestial bodies transit into this house, it can shine a light on any changes to your self-esteem or personal resources. You tend to seek security through materialistic things, but you will also wear your emotions on your sleeve.

3rd House (Gemini): House of Communication

The 3rd House represents communication, social activities, siblings, neighbors, and short-distance travel. It is ruled by the planet Mercury. As celestial bodies transit into this house, you will find that critical information concerning those closest to you is revealed. Since communication is the best way to solve most problems, allowing for a strong foundation in relationships, focusing your energy on this part of your life can lead to greater success.

4th House (Cancer): House of Home and Family

The 4th House represents home, family, self-care, femininity, and emotional foundations. It is ruled by the Moon. Celestial bodies moving through this house will implore you to put time, money, and energy into building up your infrastructure. This includes establishing safe spaces and private sanctuaries where you can work on your relationships with family members.

5th House (Leo): House of Pleasure

The 5th House represents pleasure, creativity, joy, fertility, romance, and self-expression. It is ruled by the Sun. While celestial bodies transit through this house, you will find your creative inspiration boosted, and it can greatly increase your self-confidence. Find something that fulfills you and makes you feel satisfied, no matter what that might be.

6th House (Virgo): House of Health

The 6th House represents health, fitness, habits, organization, and self-value. It is ruled by the planet Mercury. Celestial bodies moving across this house will stimulate your ability to establish good habits and redefine your daily routines. Seek a balance between your home and work life, and be sure not to neglect your mental health. Where you spend your time is just as important as who you spend that time with, so make sure you have a healthy environment around you.

7th House (Libra): House of Partnership

The 7th House, also called the Descendant, represents partnerships, relationships, marriage, contracts, equality, and interpersonal skills. It is ruled by the planet Venus. When celestial bodies move across this house, you will find success in drawing up contracts and closing major deals. Your romantic relationships are just as important as your professional ones, so if you put in the same amount of effort into them, you will achieve a significant upgrade with your partner or spouse.

8th House (Scorpio): House of Transformation

The 8th House represents transformation, assets, shared resources, intimacy, joint ventures, and mystery. It is ruled by the planet Pluto. Celestial bodies transiting this house can aid you in navigating the complex situations you might find yourself in. While it's perfectly acceptable to indulge yourself, since nobody knows just how much time they have left on this Earth, remember to remain flexible regarding your interests. You should also be willing to forgive and forget past transgressions and learn not to cling to the successes of the past. Be ready to open yourself up to the here and now and the great things that can happen in the future.

9th House (Sagittarius): House of Philosophy

The 9th House represents philosophy, higher education, travel, law, religion, learning, and transcultural relations. It is ruled by the planet Jupiter. As celestial bodies transit into this house, you will delve into a new subject enthusiastically. While you might feel stuck in a rut with your current situation, you can shake off the cobwebs and reignite your passions by looking at things differently. Sometimes a change in scenery can do just as much to break you out of a dull routine as anything else.

10th House (Capricorn): House of Social Status

The 10th House represents social status, career, long-term goals, masculinity, fame, and reputation. It is ruled by the planet Saturn. As celestial bodies move through this house, you will find yourself making a change in your career and professional aspirations. There is also a chance that it can reveal someone hiding their ambitions, possibly seeking to succeed at your expense. Be careful with who you trust, especially regarding your reputation. While being popular is not everything in life, there's no reason to let your social status needlessly suffer.

11th House (Aquarius): House of Friendship

The 11th House represents friendship, networks, technology, social awareness, humanitarianism, and community. It is ruled by the planet Uranus. Celestial bodies moving across this house will allow you to reach a wider network of people and find your place within society. Technology has made it easier to keep in touch with friends and make new professional contacts, so take advantage of its benefits. Your support system is incredibly important, and you have a solid foundation for your relationships. If you ever find yourself dealing with serious problems, you know you have good people you can lean on.

12th House (Pisces): House of Unconscious

The 12th House represents the unconscious, spirituality, healing, karma, afterlife, esotericism, and the subconscious. It is ruled by the planet Neptune. When celestial bodies transit into this house, you will discover that some people need to be removed from your life. While you are empathetic and have no problem sharing your emotions with others, some bring too much toxicity and drama to them, which is something you shouldn't feel obligated to deal with. Remember that karma will always send back to you what you put into the world, so make sure you emit positivity wherever you go.

How to Read the Kabbalistic Natal Chart

Kabbalistic natal charts are generally depicted as a wheel broken up into slices, looking a bit like a pizza pie. The wheel usually has three concentric circles, breaking each slice into three sections. The outer circle shows the twelve zodiac signs, the middle circle shows the 10 astrological planets, and the innermost circle shows the twelve astrological house numbers. Some natal charts will use symbols for each circle, while others choose to depict the zodiac signs as date ranges instead, making it easier to find someone's birth date if they aren't familiar with the zodiac. Since not all sources give the exact same date ranges for each sign, this can also avoid any confusion when plotting out someone's natal chart.

Reading a natal chart involves charting the placement of the planets in the sky at the time of your birth, as well as your geographical location. This represents the different aspects of your personality, with each planet influencing a particular trait or characteristic about you. Certain planets also rule over different zodiac signs, which gives them a stronger connection to the attributes they possess. You will also need to find the ascendant in the natal chart. The ascendant the point that was rising over the eastern horizon at the precise moment you were born, measured by sign and degree. On the natal chart wheel, this can be found on the left side, at roughly the same place where 9:00 would be located on a clock. The descendant is on the opposite side at around the location of 3:00.

The first astrological house will always match up with the ascendant. The zodiac signs and astrological planets are placed around the wheel based on the first astrological house and the ascendant. Once you have set the zodiac signs and astrological planets into their correct positions based on the time and place of your birth, you can match them up and interpret their traits and characteristics like a horoscope. Depending on the orientation of the zodiac signs and astrological planets, you might have a stronger connection to certain attributes, personality types, behaviors, incarnations, and destinies. The planets represent your actions and motivations, the astrological houses express how you complete tasks in your life, and the zodiac signs depict the aspects of yourself that you can work on to grow and change.

Examples of Natal Chart Readings

Here are some examples of natal chart readings, using all the relevant information to determine the precise date, time, and location to get a comprehensive report on the example person's traits, characteristics, personality, and life goals:

Person A (Male): Born on September 17, 1993, at 6:48 AM in New York City, New York, USA

1st House (Ascendant): Virgo - Moon, Mercury, and Jupiter

2nd House: Libra - Mars

3rd House: Scorpio - Pluto and North Node

4th House: Sagittarius - Uranus and Neptune

5th House: Capricorn - Saturn

6th House: Aquarius

7th House (Descendant): Pisces

8th House: Aries

9th House: Taurus - South Node

10th House: Gemini

11th House: Cancer - Venus

12th House: Leo - Sun

Person A has a Virgo ascendant, and the Moon is also in Virgo. The North Node is in the 3rd House, and the Sun is in Leo and the 12th House. This means they are analytical, alert, social, intelligent, erudite, reserved, critical, helpful, and conscientious. They're the type of person who is a great public speaker but can put a bit too much pressure on others to live up to their standards. Likely career paths include politician, professor, lecturer, or social activist.

Person B (Female): Born on May 25, 1977, at 3:04 PM in Paris, France

1st House (Ascendant): Cancer
2nd House: Leo - Saturn
3rd House: Leo
4th House: Virgo - Pluto and North Node
5th House: Libra - Moon and Uranus
6th House: Sagittarius - Neptune
7th House (Descendant): Capricorn - Mercury and Mars
8th House: Aquarius - Sun
9th House: Aquarius
10th House: Pisces - Venus and South Node
11th House: Aries - Jupiter
12th House: Gemini

Person B has a Cancer ascendant. The North Node is in Virgo and the 4th House. The Moon is in the 5th House, and the Sun is in the 8th House. This means they are brave, independent, sensual, progressive, independent, and autonomous. They have an unusual, rebellious, and revolutionary spirit, as well as strong ideals and great courage in the face of adversity. Likely career paths include artist, social activist, journalist, or romance author.

Person C (Non-Binary): Born on June 26, 2001, at 10:31 PM in Tokyo, Japan

1st House (Ascendant): Pisces
2nd House: Aries - Venus
3rd House: Taurus - Saturn
4th House: Gemini - Sun, Mercury, Jupiter, and North Node
5th House: Cancer
6th House: Leo
7th House (Descendant): Virgo - Moon
8th House: Libra

9th House: Scorpio – Pluto

10th House: Sagittarius – Mars and South Node

11th House: Capricorn

12th House: Aquarius – Uranus and Neptune

Person C has a Pisces ascendant. The Sun and North Node are in Gemini and the 4th House. The Moon is in Virgo and the 7th House. This means they are tenacious, calm, tender, discreet, thoughtful, sensitive, humble, and impressionable. They have a strong sense of individuality, radiant, creative energy, very good memory, and strict emotional discipline. However, they can also be somewhat timid, indecisive, anxious, lazy, or manipulative. Likely, careers include scientist, doctor, surgeon, medical researcher, scholar, academic, or health care worker.

Chapter 9: Kabbalah and the Tarot Cards

The history of Kabbalah and Tarot are more closely intertwined than many people realize. While various sources give different dates of inception for Tarot, including Ancient Egypt, 13th century France, or 15th century Italy, one of the first definitive guides to Tarot was published by Kabbalist Eliphas Levi in 1856. The Dogme et Rituel de la Haute Magie (Dogma and Ritual of High Magic) was split into 22 chapters, mirroring the 22 cards of Tarot's Major Arcana. He also equated each Major Arcana card with a letter of the Hebrew alphabet and the four suits of the Minor Arcana with the Tetragrammaton.

In 1889, Levi's student, Gerard Encausse, published his own book focusing on Tarot under the name "Papus," titling it The Tarot of the Bohemians. Around the same time, the Swiss occultist Oswald Wirth put out the first deck of Major Arcana cards that incorporated the 22 Hebrew letters into their traditional designs. The Golden Dawn also utilized the Hebrew alphabet in their Tarot decks, even though they didn't print the letters on the cards themselves. Writings from members of the organization show that members assigned the sephirot to the ten numbered cards of the Minor Arcana and the Four Worlds to the four suits. Aleister Crowley even swapped the letters connected to the Major Arcana cards known as The Emperor and the Star, giving "Tsadi" to the Emperor and "He" to the Star.

Both Kabbalah and Tarot also share basic tenets in their belief systems. The four suits of the Tarot deck refer to different aspects of a person's life – the suit of Swords equates to knowledge, Wands to sexuality and passion, Cups to emotions, and Pentacles to money and careers. This correlates to the way the sephirot of the Tree of Life and Kabbalistic astrology express similar attributes when assigned to a person's life. The 22 cards of the Major Arcana have been equated with the 22 paths of the sephirot in the Tree of Life and the 22 letters of the Hebrew alphabet.

The Tarot Card System

The modern Kabbalistic Tarot card deck has 78 cards. There are 22 Major Arcana cards, each with its own name and associated traits, and 56 Minor Arcana cards. The Minor Arcana cards are divided into 4 suits, with 14 cards per suit. Each suit contains numbered cards, from 1 to 10, and 4 court cards, including the King, Queen, Knight, and Page. The 4 suits are named Swords, Wands, Cups, and Pentacles. Tarot cards can be used for cartomancy or the art of a special form of divination utilizing a deck of cards. In addition to fortune-telling, they can reveal all kinds of information that can help you find out more about yourself. This is referenced by the names of the two sets in the Tarot deck: Major Arcana means "greater secrets," and Minor Arcana means "lesser secrets."

Major Arcana Tarot Cards

The 22 Major Arcana Tarot cards are known as the named, numbered, or trump cards. They are generally assigned a standardized name and number combination, using Roman numerals for each one. However, the Fool card carries no number on its face, so the numerals only range from 1 to 21, rendered as I to XXI. Although the Fool can be placed at the top or the bottom of the set of named cards, unofficially giving it the number 0 (zero) or XXII (22), Kabbalistic Tarot decks usually assign it to the top and consider it numbered as 0.

Major arcana Tarot cards.
https://unsplash.com/photos/y3qrbAgm7q8

List of Cards

1. **The Fool (0):** Assigned the Hebrew letter Aleph. It is associated with the planet Uranus, the element of Air, and the zodiac sign of Aquarius. In different Tarot card systems, the Fool can either be placed first or last, but in Kabbalistic versions of the deck, it's always placed first. Although the card itself doesn't have a number on it, the Fool is considered the number zero when placed first or XXII (22) when placed last. This card depicts a man dressed in stereotypical foolish attire. When the card is upright, it represents adventure, innocence, and new beginnings. If it is reversed, it means recklessness, fearlessness, and taking unnecessary risks.

2. **The Magician (I):** Assigned the Hebrew letter Bet. It is associated with the planet Mercury, the element of Air, and the zodiac sign of Gemini. Typically, this card shows the figure of the Magician pointing upward with one hand and downwards with the other. This is taken to represent the phrase "as above, so below," often interpreted as meaning that whatever is created in the metaphysical realm will manifest in the physical world. The card also shows a table with a sword, wand, cup, and pentacle, which are the four suits of the Minor Arcana. When the card is upright,

it represents willpower, creation, and manifestation. If it is reversed, it means manipulation, wasted talents, and a lack of foresight.

3. **The High Priestess (II):** Assigned the Hebrew letter Gimel. It is associated with the Moon, the element of Water, and the zodiac sign of Cancer. This card depicts a woman wearing blue robes in a seated position with her hands on her lap. There is a crescent moon at her feet, and she wears a horned crown on her head. She sits between a white pillar and a black pillar, which symbolizes duality. When the card is upright, it represents feminine divinity, intuition, and the unconscious. If it is reversed, it means silence, withdrawal, and repressed emotions.

4. **The Empress (III):** Assigned the Hebrew letter Dalet. It is associated with the planet Venus, the element of Fire, and the zodiac sign of Taurus. This card depicts a woman sitting on a throne and wearing a crown with twelve stars on top of it, symbolizing the twelve zodiac signs, twelve astrological houses, and twelve months of the year. She also holds a scepter in one hand, showing the power she holds over life. When the card is upright, it represents fertility, nourishment, abundance, and femininity. If it is reversed, it means emptiness, overbearing, and dependence.

5. **The Emperor (IV):** Assigned the Hebrew letter He (or Tsadi). It is associated with the planet Mars, the element of Fire, and the zodiac sign of Aries. This card depicts a regal-looking man sitting upon a throne adorned with ram heads. He wears a cloak and has a long, white beard, holding a scepter shaped like an Ankh in his right hand and a globe in his left hand. When the card is upright, it represents authority, structure, establishment, and paternal feelings. If it is reversed, it means inflexibility, domination, undisciplined, and excessive overt control.

6. **The Hierophant (V):** Assigned the Hebrew letter Vav. It is associated with the planet Venus, the element of Earth, and the zodiac sign of Taurus. This card depicts a religious leader holding his right hand aloft, with two fingers pointing up and two pointing down, symbolizing a bridge between Heaven and Hell. He has a triple cross-staff in his left hand and wears a triple-tiered crown. The Hierophant is positioned between two pillars, with

one showing Obedience and the other Disobedience. When the card is upright, it represents tradition, ethics, morality, conformity, and spiritual wisdom. If it is reversed, it means subversiveness, freedom, rebellion, and personal beliefs.

7. **The Lovers (VI):** Assigned the Hebrew letter Zayin. It is associated with the planet Mercury, the element of Air, and the zodiac sign of Gemini. This card depicts a man and a woman (sometimes Adam and Eve) standing on opposite sides of an angelic figure looming overhead in the middle. When the card is upright, it represents love, harmony, partnerships, and decisions. If it is reversed, it means inequity, disharmony, powerlessness, and instability.

8. **The Chariot (VII):** Assigned the Hebrew letter Het. It is associated with the Moon, the element of Water, and the zodiac sign of Cancer. This card depicts a man in a chariot being pulled by a pair of horses or sphinxes, one colored black and the other white. He is wearing a crown or helmet and a set of stylized armor. The man is not holding any reins but is sometimes shown with a sword or wand in his hand. When upright, the card represents success, determination, control, direction, action, and strength of will. If it is reversed, it means opposition, inconsistency, and unreliability.

9. **Strength (VIII):** Assigned the Hebrew letter Tet. It is associated with the Sun, the element of Fire, and the zodiac sign of Leo. This card depicts a woman leaning over a lion, sometimes grabbing his jaws. Some versions show the infinity symbol above her head. When the card is upright, it represents strength, bravery, compassion, persuasiveness, focus, and influence. If it is reversed, it means weakness, insecurity, lethargy, and un-tempered emotions.

10. **The Hermit (IX):** Assigned the Hebrew letter Yod. It is associated with the planet Mercury, the element of Earth, and the zodiac sign of Virgo. This card is depicted as a cloaked and hooded old man standing atop a mountain. He has a staff in one hand and a lit lantern in the other, with the light coming from a six-pointed star. The light of the lantern symbolizes guidance into the unknown. When the card is upright, it represents solitude, wisdom, spiritual enlightenment, and passion. If it is reversed, it

means loneliness, terror, anxiety, sadness, and depression.

11. **Wheel of Fortune (X):** Assigned the Hebrew letter Kaf. It is associated with the planet Jupiter, the element of Fire, and the zodiac sign of Capricorn. This card typically depicts a wheel or compass face, and it is sometimes inscribed with the letters T-A-R-O when reading clockwise from the top. There are usually figures, animals, and other ornamentation surrounding the wheel. When upright, the card represents chance, destiny, fate, karma, turning points, and life cycles. If it is reversed, it means upheaval, unwanted change, obstacles, and being at the whim of outside forces.

12. **Justice (XI):** Assigned the Hebrew letter Lamed. It is associated with the planet Venus, the element of Air, and the zodiac sign of Libra. This card depicts a seated figure, such as a king or a judge, holding a sword in their right hand and a golden scale in their left hand. The scale symbolizes a fair and balanced decision. When the card is upright, it represents justice, integrity, legitimacy, rationality, civility, and life lessons. If it is reversed, it means injustice, fraud, irresponsibility, dishonesty, disloyalty, criminality, or acts of evil.

13. **The Hanged Man (XII):** Assigned the Hebrew letter Mem. It is associated with the planet Venus, the element of Earth, and the zodiac sign of Taurus. This card depicts a man hanging upside-down from a tree or the gallows, secured there by one foot. He is sometimes given a golden halo to symbolize martyrdom, atonement, or enlightenment. When the card is upright, it represents sacrifice, self-reflection, uncertainty, liberation, and spiritual development. If it is reversed, it means selfishness, stagnation, bad habits, and an unsolvable problem.

14. **Death (XIII):** Assigned the Hebrew letter, Nun. It is associated with the planet Pluto, the element of Water, and the zodiac sign of Scorpio. This card depicts the Grim Reaper wielding a scythe. He is sometimes shown wearing a suit of black armor and riding atop a pale horse. When upright, the card represents rebirth, transformation, modesty, powerful movement, simplification, and the end of a cycle. It means fear of new beginnings, restrictiveness, small-mindedness, and resistance to change if it is reversed.

15. **Temperance (XIV):** Assigned the Hebrew letter Samekh. It is associated with the planet Jupiter, the element of Fire, and the zodiac sign of Sagittarius. This card depicts a winged angel with a triangle inside a square on its chest. Just above these shapes is the Tetragrammaton. The angel has one foot on land and the other in water. When the card is upright, it represents balance, moderation, cooperation, and problem-solving. If it is reversed, it means imbalance, discord, overindulgence, carelessness, and audacity.

16. **The Devil (XV):** Assigned the Hebrew letter Ayin. It is associated with the planet Saturn, the element of Earth, and the zodiac sign of Capricorn. This card depicts a large demonic figure on a pedestal with ram horns, bat wings, and the feet of a harpy. There is an upside-down pentagram on his forehead; his right hand is raised while his left is lowered and holding a torch. There is a pair of unclothed demons with tails, one of whom is male and the other female, both chained to the pedestal. When upright, the card represents betrayal, depression, addiction, captivity, negativity, and a focus on material things. It means freedom, independence, detachment, overcoming addiction, and a reclamation of power if it is reversed.

17. **The Tower (XVI):** Assigned the Hebrew letter Pe. It is associated with the planet Mars, the element of Fire, and the zodiac sign of Aries. This card depicts a large tower being struck by lightning and set ablaze while two people are either fleeing from an open door or leaping out of the flame-engulfed windows. When upright, the card represents release, tragedy, revelations, loss, and a sudden change. It means avoiding tragedy, resisting change, delaying the inevitable, and narrowly escaping danger if it is reversed.

18. **The Star (XVII):** Assigned the Hebrew letter Tsadi (or He). It is associated with the planet Uranus, the element of Air, and the zodiac sign of Aquarius. This card depicts an unclothed woman kneeling by the water, with one foot in the water and the other on land. She has a pair of jugs in her hands, pouring liquid into the water and onto the land. A large star is floating above her head, and seven smaller stars symbolizing the seven chakras are positioned around it. When the card is upright, it represents hope, recuperation, renewal, generosity, creativity, and

inspiration. If it is reversed, it means despair, boredom, hopelessness, discouragement, and a lack of creativity or inspiration.

19. **The Moon (XVIII):** Assigned the Hebrew letter Qof. It is associated with the planet Neptune, the element of Water, and the zodiac sign of Pisces. This card depicts a scene at night where a wild wolf and a domesticated dog are both howling at the moon. The moon has sixteen larger rays and sixteen smaller rays, as well as fifteen dew drops falling from it. There are two pillars on opposite sides of the card, and water near the bottom of the card with a crayfish emerging onto the land. When the card is upright, it represents confusion, fear, anxiety, delusion, and risk. If it is reversed, it means clarity, beating anxiety, overcoming fear, and uncovering the truth.

20. **The Sun (XIX):** Assigned the Hebrew letter, Resh. It is associated with the Sun, the element of Fire, and the zodiac sign of Leo. This card depicts an anthropomorphized sun with long rays being emitted from it and a row of sunflowers beneath it. There is a baby riding a white steed and holding a red banner or flag, symbolizing the blood of renewal. When the card is upright, it represents success, happiness, truth, fertility, and optimism. If it is reversed, it means failure, procrastination, sadness, and lies.

21. **Judgment (XX):** Assigned the Hebrew letter, Shin. It is associated with the planet Pluto and the element of Fire but has no corresponding zodiac sign. This card depicts a large, looming angel near the top who is blowing a trumpet with the flag of St. George hanging from it. The angel is sometimes said to be Metatron and a scene from the Book of Revelations. A group of ashy, sallow people is standing around, looking up at the angel with their arms extending toward him. They symbolize the resurrected emerging from their graves. When upright, the card represents rebirth, awakening, reflection, absolution, reckoning, and a spiritual calling. If it is reversed, it means uncertainty, insecurity, indecision, despondency, and melancholy.

22. **The World (XXI):** Assigned the Hebrew letter Tav. It is associated with the planet Saturn and the element of Earth but has no corresponding zodiac sign. This card depicts an unclothed woman dancing above the Earth. She is encircled by

either a wreath or an ouroboros eating its own tail. There are figures in the four corners of the card - a man in the top left, an eagle in the top right, an ox in the bottom left, and a lion in the bottom right. When the card is upright, it represents unity, integration, fulfillment, completion, and a great journey. If it is reversed, it means emptiness, incompletion, shortcuts, delays, and confinement.

Kabbalistic Principles of Major Arcana Tarot Cards

In Kabbalah, the Major Arcana Tarot cards have a special esoteric significance. They are considered to be a "Bible of Bibles," capable of revealing every truth within all of creation. Since each named card of the Major Arcana has specific traits and characteristics associated with them, when performing a reading, they can unveil the secrets of a person's soul and uncover the mysteries of the past, present, and future. The archetypes depicted on each card represent the various forms of the world's human and divine aspects. There is a careful balance between the conscious and subconscious, the physical and metaphysical realms, positive and negative emotions, good and evil, and Man and God.

Connection to the 22 Paths

Kabbalah introduces a connection to the sephirot and the Tree of Life to the Major Arcana Tarot cards. Each named card is associated with a specific path along the Tree corresponding to its standard attributes. There are three distinct subsets of sephirotic paths within the Tree of Life: the column on the right is called the Pillar of Mercy, which embodies the positive, active, and male side. The column on the left is called the Pillar of Judgment and possesses the negative, passive, and female sides. The column in the middle is called the Pillar of Harmony, and it reconciles the two opposing sides by bringing them into balance.

The Major Arcana Tarot cards and their associated sephirot paths include:

1. **The Fool:** Keter to Chochmah (Pillar of Mercy)
2. **The Magician:** Keter to Binah (Pillar of Judgment)
3. **The High Priestess:** Keter to Tiferet (Pillar of Harmony)
4. **The Empress:** Chochmah to Binah (Pillar of Harmony)
5. **The Emperor:** Chochmah to Tiferet (Pillar of Mercy)

6. **The Hierophant:** Chochmah to Chesed (Pillar of Mercy)
7. **The Lovers:** Binah to Tiferet (Pillar of Judgment)
8. **The Chariot:** Binah to Geburah (Pillar of Judgment)
9. **Strength**: Chesed to Geburah (Pillar of Harmony)
10. **The Hermit:** Chesed to Tiferet (Pillar of Mercy)
11. **The Wheel of Fortune:** Chesed to Netsach (Pillar of Mercy)
12. **Justice:** Geburah to Tiferet (Pillar of Judgment)
13. **The Hanged Man:** Geburah to Hod (Pillar of Judgment)
14. **Death:** Tiferet to Netsach (Pillar of Mercy)
15. **Temperance:** Tiferet to Yesod (Pillar of Harmony)
16. **The Devil:** Hod to Tiferet (Pillar of Judgment)
17. **The Tower:** Netsach to Hod (Pillar of Harmony)
18. **The Star:** Yesod to Netsach (Pillar of Mercy)
19. **The Moon:** Netsach to Malkuth (Pillar of Mercy)
20. **The Sun:** Yesod to Hod (Pillar of Judgment)
21. **Judgment:** Hod to Malkuth (Pillar of Judgment)
22. **The World:** Malkuth to Yesod (Pillar of Harmony)

Minor Arcana Tarot Cards

The 56 Minor Arcana Tarot cards are the suit cards in a Tarot deck. They have 4 suits, each with cards numbered from 1 to 10. These cards are either unillustrated, only having pips denoting their number and suit, or will carry a thematically-consistent design. Some decks will use an Ace in place of the number 1, while others just use its actual number. There are also 4 court or face cards in each suit. These are generally given as King, Queen, Knight, and Page, but some versions will replace the Page with a Jack or Knave. The suits used are typically Swords, Wands, Cups, and Pentacles, but some decks will swap Swords with Blades or Spades; Wands with Staves, Clubs, or Batons; Cups with Chalices, Goblets, Hearts, or Vessels; and Pentacles with Coins, Rings, Diamonds, or Disks.

List of Cards

The suit of Swords represents actions, words, and thoughts:
1. **One (Ace) of Swords**: When upright, this card means triumph, conquest, and great prosperity. If reversed, it refers to hatred,

failure, and great misery.

2. **Two of Swords:** When upright, this card means meditation, inner harmony, and balanced decisions. If reversed, it refers to blindness, fear, and rash decisions.

3. **Three of Swords:** When upright, this card means deep sorrow, lost relationships, and accidental death. If reversed, it refers to mitigated sorrow, missed connections, and premeditated murder.

4. **Four of Swords:** When upright, this card means vigilance, solitude, exile, coffin, and tomb. If reversed, it refers to precaution, avarice, testament, circumspection, economy, and wise administration.

5. **Five of Swords**: When upright, this card means confidence, potency, preparation, and victory. If reversed, it refers to the dangers of overconfidence or a victory that seems assured *turning into a defeat.*

6. **Six of Swords:** When upright, this card means movement, long journeys, escape from danger, fleeing from problems, relief from pain, and gradual change. If reversed, it refers to immobility, moving toward danger, endless pain, and sudden change.

7. **Seven of Swords:** When upright, this card means mind, intellect, and diplomacy over violence. If reversed, it refers to overthinking, surrender, and disinterest in solving a problem.

8. **Eight of Swords:** When upright, this card means impossible situations, sacrifice, and enduring pain to escape a trap. If reversed, it refers to the fear of acting, hesitancy to speak up, and acceptance of captivity.

9. **Nine of Swords:** When upright, this card means premonitions, deception, nightmares, depression, suffering, scandal, violence, disappointment, and cruelty. If reversed, it refers to unfounded fears, guilt, doubt, distrust, misery, malice, suspicion, imprisonment, and isolation.

10. **Ten of Swords**: When upright, this card means bleak situations, mental anguish, and temporary destruction. If reversed, it refers to long-term problems, finding the silver lining, and tempering despair to safeguard future opportunities for success.

11. **Page of Swords**: When upright, this card means curiosity, moving freely, and strong energy. If reversed, it refers to hindered

movement, encumbrance, and indolence.

12. **Knight of Swords:** When upright, this card means foolish courage, clever liars, confident tricksters, and secrets. If reversed, it refers to reconsidering actions, avoiding mistakes, and remaining faithful.
13. **Queen of Swords:** When upright, this card means freedom of speech, unfiltered thoughts, active intelligence, and clarity of mind. If reversed, it refers to clouded thoughts, censorship, and dimwittedness.
14. **King of Swords:** When upright, this card means decisive, reasonable, understanding, and stout of heart. If reversed, it refers to ruthlessness, excessive judgment, and un-enlightenment.

The suit of Wands represents passion, motivation, and energy:

1. **One (Ace) of Wands**: When upright, this card means birth, ambition, creativity, good fortune, commencement, inventiveness, and new beginnings. If reversed, it refers to delayed progress, loss of wealth, illness, and greed.
2. **Two of Wands:** When upright, this card means achievement, boldness, partnership, and goals. If reversed, it refers to anxiety, doubt, meekness, and playing it safe.
3. **Three of Wands:** When upright, this card means long-term success, traveling, fresh starts, trade, and adventure. It refers to cessation, disappointment, toiling, and ending a task if reversed.
4. **Four of Wands:** When upright, this card means harmony, prosperity, celebrations, pleasure, and happiness. If reversed, it refers to transience, burdens, lack of support, conflict at home, and feeling unwelcome.
5. **Five of Wands**: When upright, this card means aggression, tension, conflict, rivalry, competition, arguments, and disagreement. It refers to cooperation, truce, peace, and resolving or avoiding conflict if reversed.
6. **Six of Wands:** When upright, this card means triumph, confidence, rewards, praise, recognition, acclaim, and pride. It refers to failure, feeling overlooked, financial loss, poor investments, and working without recognition if reversed.
7. **Seven of Wands:** When upright, this card means self-defense, protection, fighting for love, beating the odds, and undertaking a

challenge. If reversed, it refers to yielding your ground, surrendering, defensiveness, losing a competition, or failure due to overconfidence.
8. **Eight of Wands:** When upright, this card means swiftness, snap decisions, excitement, speed, and progress. If reversed, it refers to misunderstanding, chaos, hastiness, waiting, unpreparedness, and sloth.
9. **Nine of Wands**: When upright, this card means persistence, perseverance, resilience, grit, fatigue, and last stands. If reversed, it refers to defensiveness, stubbornness, rigidity, and a refusal to compromise.
10. **Ten of Wands:** When upright, this card means responsibility, duty, obligation, struggling, burdens, stress, and burning out. If reversed, it refers to breakdown, collapse, taking on too much responsibility, and inability to delegate.
11. **Page of Wands:** When upright, this card means excitement, cheerfulness, adventure, extroversion, energy, and new ideas. If reversed, it refers to impatience, tantrums, boredom, laziness, distractions, and unreliability.
12. **Knight of Wands:** When upright, this card means charm, rebellion, heroism, courage, energy, hot-tempered, and free spirits. If reversed, it refers to recklessness, arrogance, impatience, passivity, volatility, and domination.
13. **Queen of Wands**: When upright, this card means confidence, charisma, determination, optimism, self-assuredness, vivaciousness, and sociability. If reversed, it refers to vengeance, jealousy, temperamentality, demand, selfishness, timidity, and bullying.
14. **King of Wands:** When upright, this card means vision, leadership, boldness, taking control, and looking at the big picture. If reversed, it refers to tyranny, viciousness, powerlessness, forcefulness, ineffectiveness, and weakness.

The suit of Cups represents feelings, emotions, creativity, and intuition:
1. **One (Ace) of Cups:** When upright, this card means love, creativity, spirituality, emotional awakening, intuition, and new feelings. If reversed, it refers to emptiness, frigidity, gloominess,

emotional loss, feeling unloved, and a creative block.

2. **Two of Cups:** When upright, this card means attraction, unity, mutual respect, partnership, connection, and forging close bonds. If reversed, it refers to rejection, imbalance, separation, tension, withdrawal, division, and poor communication.

3. **Three of Cups:** When upright, this card means community, friendship, gatherings, celebrations, social events, and group activities. If reversed, it refers to excessiveness, scandal, gossip, loneliness, isolation, solitude, and social imbalance.

4. **Four of Cups:** When upright, this card means apathy, melancholy, boredom, contemplation, discontentedness, indifference, and feeling disconnected. If reversed, it refers to awareness, negativity, clarity, acceptance, depression, and opting for happiness.

5. **Five of Cups:** When upright, this card means sadness, grief, loss, disappointment, mourning, and feeling discontent. If reversed, it refers to acceptance, contentment, moving on, positivity, and achieving inner peace.

6. **Six of Cups:** When upright, this card means nostalgia, sentimentality, familiarity, memories, comfort, healing, and pleasure. If reversed, it refers to independence, leaving home, moving forward, and being stuck in the past.

7. **Seven of Cups:** When upright, this card means illusion, daydreams, fantasy, choices, wishful thinking, indecision, and seeking a purpose. If reversed, it refers to distraction, diversion, disarray, clarity, feeling adrift, and making a choice.

8. **Eight of Cups:** When upright, this card means seeking truth, abandonment, letting go, escapism, and choosing happiness over money. If reversed, it refers to stagnation, avoidance, monotony, fearing change, acceptance of loss, and remaining in a bad situation.

9. **Nine of Cups:** When upright, this card means contentment, success, recognition, satisfaction, achievement, pleasure, and wish fulfillment. If reversed, it refers to disappointment, unhappiness, arrogance, underachievement, snobbery, and lacking fulfillment.

10. **Ten of Cups:** When upright, this card means homecoming, security, happiness, emotional stability, and domestic harmony.

If reversed, it refers to separation, disharmony, isolation, and domestic conflict.

11. **Page of Cups:** When upright, this card means sensitivity, naivete, idealism, innocence, a dreamer, and one's inner child. If reversed, it refers to immaturity, insecurity, escapism, emotional vulnerability, and neglecting your inner child.

12. **Knight of Cups:** When upright, this card means charm, artistry, gracefulness, idealism, tactfulness, diplomacy, mediation, and negotiation. If reversed, it refers to moodiness, disappointment, turmoil, vanity, throwing tantrums, and avoiding conflict.

13. **Queen of Cups:** When upright, this card means warmth, compassion, kindness, supportiveness, intuition, counseling, and healing. If reversed, it refers to insecurity, neediness, fragility, martyrdom, dependence, oversharing, and excessively sensitive.

14. **King of Cups:** When upright, this card means wisdom, diplomacy, advisor, devotion, and striking a balance between your head and heart. If reversed, it refers to anxiety, coldness, repression, withdrawal, manipulation, selfishness, and feeling overwhelmed.

The suit of Pentacles represents work, finances, and material possessions:

1. **One (Ace) of Pentacles:** When upright, this card means resourcefulness, abundance, security, prosperity, stability, manifestation, and new opportunities. If reversed, it refers to scarcity, instability, deficiency, stinginess, missed chances, and poor investments.

2. **Two of Pentacles:** When upright, this card means adaptation, flexibility, resourcefulness, and balancing or stretching resources. If reversed, it refers to disorganization, imbalance, messiness, chaos, overextension, and feeling overwhelmed.

3. **Three of Pentacles:** When upright, this card means teamwork, collaboration, effort, apprenticeship, combined goals, and shared energy. If reversed, it refers to apathy, conflict, egotism, idleness, competition, disunity, and lacking cohesion.

4. **Four of Pentacles:** When upright, this card means possessiveness, stinginess, hoarding, security, materialism, savings, frugality, accumulated wealth, boundaries, and

guardedness. If reversed, it refers to generosity, recklessness, insecurity, reckless spending, vulnerability, and financial mismanagement.

5. **Five of Pentacles:** When upright, this card means hardship, loss, adversity, isolation, disgrace, alienation, unemployment, struggles, and feeling abandoned. If reversed, it refers to forgiveness, overcoming adversity, recovering from loss, positive changes, and welcomeness.

6. **Six of Pentacles:** When upright, this card means charity, community, support, gratitude, sharing, generosity, and transactions. If reversed, it refers to inequity, extortion, abusing generosity, power dynamics, and gifts with strings attached.

7. **Seven of Pentacles:** When upright, this card means progress, growth, rewards, harvest, results, perseverance, planning, and patience. If reversed, it refers to waste, setbacks, impatience, procrastination, stagnation, lack of effort, unfinished work, or unrewarded effort.

8. **Eight of Pentacles:** When upright, this card means craftsmanship, skill, talent, quality, expertise, mastery, dedication, accomplishment, commitment, and high standards. If reversed, it refers to laziness, ill-repute, poor quality, unskilled, demotivation, and being stuck in a dead-end job.

9. **Nine of Pentacles:** When upright, this card means success, independence, achievement, leisure, self-sufficiency, financial security, and rewarded efforts. If reversed, it refers to reckless spending, superficiality, financial instability, guardedness, and living beyond your means.

10. **Ten of Pentacles:** When upright, this card means ancestry, legacy, family, roots, inheritance, foundation, privilege, affluence, tradition, and stability. If reversed, it refers to bankruptcy, debt, instability, familial disputes, financial conflict, and breaking tradition.

11. **Page of Pentacles:** When upright, this card means ambition, diligence, planning, consistency, studiousness, loyalty, faithfulness, dependability, and groundedness. If reversed, it refers to foolishness, immaturity, irresponsibility, procrastination, laziness, underachievement, and missed chances.

12. **Knight of Pentacles**: When upright, this card means practicality, efficiency, reliability, commitment, patience, reliability, conservative, and steadfastness. If reversed, it refers to boredom, irresponsibility, gambling, indifference, and being a workaholic.

13. **Queen of Pentacles**: When upright, this card means nurturing, caring, sensibility, practicality, welcoming, luxuriousness, being a homebody, and a good head for business. If reversed, it refers to selfishness, jealousy, insecurity, greed, unkemptness, materialism, intolerance, envy, self-absorption, and shallowness.

14. **King of Pentacles**: When upright, this card means prosperity, ambition, abundance, safety, kindness, protectiveness, providing sensuality, reliability, security, business acumen, and patriarchy. If reversed, it refers to materialism, greed, wastefulness, exploitativeness, possessiveness, chauvinism, and poor investments.

Kabbalistic Principles of Minor Arcana Tarot Cards

In Kabbalah, the Minor Arcana Tarot cards represent the more mundane aspects of your life. The court cards symbolize the types of people you will meet on a day-to-day basis. Swords embody nobles and military personnel, Wands depict artisans and craftsmen, Cups reference the clergy, and Pentacles show merchants, vendors, and traders. The ten numbered cards can also be equated with the ten sephirot in the Tree of Life and their primary attributes. This includes:

- **Ones (Aces):** Keter – Crown (Point)
- **Twos:** Chochmah – Wisdom (Force)
- **Threes:** Binah – Understanding (Form)
- **Fours:** Chesed – Love or Mercy (Expanding)
- **Fives:** Geburah – Strength (Organizing)
- **Sixes:** Tiferet – Beauty (Awareness)
- **Sevens:** Netsach – Victory (Emotions)
- **Eights:** Hod – Glory (The Mind)
- **Nines:** Yesod – Foundation (The Psyche)
- **Tens:** Malkuth – Kingdom (Activity)

The Four Suits and the Kabbalistic Worlds

Each Minor Arcana suit corresponds to the Four Worlds from the Kabbalistic Tree of Life. They also have a connection to different aspects of the metaphysical realms and facets of life. These include:

- **Swords:** Yetzirah – Formation (Thinking)
- **Wands:** Atziluth – Emanation (Spirit)
- **Cups:** Beriah – Creation (Feeling)
- **Pentacles**: Assiah – Action (Doing)

Kabbalah delves into the secrets of the hidden world, and the correlation between the Minor Arcana suits and the Four Worlds, combined with the numbered cards and sephirot, are expressed through specific verses and keywords by using the prompts of "Life is..." or "Creation is..." For example:

- The Four of Swords would be associated with the sephirah of Chesed and the world of Yetzirah. Translated through the corresponding attributes, this would be rendered as "Life is expanding your thinking." This can be adjusted to read, "Life is a growth of your mindset."
- The Ten of Pentacles is associated with the sephirah of Malkuth and the world of Assiah. It would be rendered as "Creation is the activity of doing," or when adjusted, it becomes "Creation is the act of doing."
- The Seven Cups are associated with Netsach and Beriah. It would be rendered as "Life is emotions you are feeling" or "Life is experiencing the gamut of emotions."
- The Six Wands are associated with Tiferet and Atziluth. This is rendered as "Life is an awareness of your spirit" or "Life has a spiritual awakening."

Tarot and the Tetragrammaton

The Tetragrammaton, or the four Hebrew letters that make up the name of God, can be associated with the four suits in the Minor Arcana. Since each card in the Major Arcana is assigned a Hebrew letter, they also correspond to the Tetragrammaton. It is usually rendered as Yod-He-Vav-He (יהוה). Those who can learn how to properly pronounce this name are said to possess the power to release all hidden and arcane knowledge in the universe.

When connecting the Tetragrammaton to the Minor Arcana, you need to look at the numerical values of each Hebrew letter: Yod is 10, He is 5, and Vav is 6.

Therefore, the cards chosen to represent it would be:

the 10 of Swords,

5 of Wands,

6 of Cups,

5 of Pentacles

Rendered using the sephirot and Four Worlds combinations, it would be:

Malkuth and Yetzirah

Geburah and Atziluth

Tiferet and Beriah

Geburah and Assiah

Taking the Major Arcana cards related to the Tetragrammaton, you would have the Hermit for Yod, the Emperor for He, the Hierophant for Vav, and the Emperor for He again. These can be combined with the Four Worlds, just like the Minor Arcana cards, or they can be taken alone, looking at the associated paths along the Tree of Life. Interestingly, they all involve the same three sephirot: Chochmah, Chesed, and Tiferet. The Hermit is paired with Chesed to Tiferet, the Emperor with Chochmah to Tiferet, and the Hierophant with Chochmah to Chesed.

When looking at a diagram of the Tree of Light, you can see that these three paths create the shape of an irregular triangle in the upper right portion. Three is a sacred number in Kabbalah, just as it is in Judaism, Islam, and Christianity. There are three parts to the Torah, three patriarchs, and three angels visited Abraham, and the Jewish people are meant to pray three times a day. The twelve tribes of Israel were arrayed into four equal groups consisting of three tribes each when around the Tabernacle. This reflects how the Tetragrammaton uses three individual Hebrew letters in a set of four to spell out the name of God.

Chapter 10: Qabalistic Tarot Reading

Now that you understand the individual cards of the Tarot deck and what they represent, it's time to learn how to actually perform a reading with them. Readings are the method used to uncover the secrets about yourself and your life, making them a key component of Kabbalah and Tarot. Without knowing how to properly perform a reading, everything else concerning a Tarot deck is effectively useless. This is something that requires plenty of practice - nobody gets it exactly right on their first try, so don't feel discouraged if it takes time before you start to get the hang of it. Performing a truly comprehensive reading involves years of careful study to master, but you can learn how to do a relatively basic reading far quicker than that.

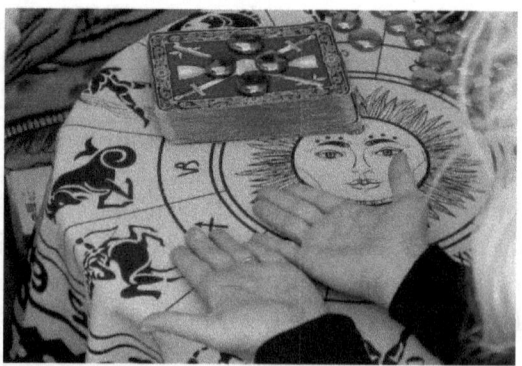

It takes practice and focus to be able to read the Tarots properly.
https://unsplash.com/photos/Ka-speuU7W4

Preparing a Reading

Making the right preparations before attempting a reading is necessary to ensure success. If you don't follow these steps, it will throw off the entire process, leaving any results open to error and misinterpretation. The main thing you need to remember is to always stay focused. Don't let your attention wander because while preparing your deck, there will be a connection between your mind, body, and spirit. Even your emotional state can influence a reading, so try to remain calm and collected as you prepare.

Choose Your Deck

The first thing you must do is choose your deck. Make sure it has all 78 cards with the right Major and Minor Arcana cards, as laid out in the previous chapter. A popular choice for Kabbalists is the Rider-Waite deck, which features the correct setup and has iconic artwork most often associated with Tarot. Your decision here is important since which specific cards you have in your deck will determine the traits and characteristics available when performing a reading.

Shuffle the Cards

After you have your chosen Tarot cards deck, you must shuffle them thoroughly. However, this isn't the same as shuffling playing cards. While shuffling, you must meditate on the areas of your life where you seek more clarity. This is part of the mystical aspect of Tarot reading. By thinking about the answers, you want, you will emit that energy using the deck as a conduit and manifest the results by imbuing each card with that metaphysical energy. You also need to decide if you want to include reversed cards. These have different meanings associated with them, and if you would like to include them, you need to alter the manner in which you shuffle the deck to randomize the orientation of each card by turning some 180 degrees.

Clear and Reset the Deck

If you've used the Tarot deck to perform a reading before, you need to clear and reset them. This involves reshuffling at least once but usually will take multiple shuffles to get right. The objective is to remove any residual energy from your previous reading, as having "tainted" cards will negatively impact your next attempt. An easy way to ensure your cards have been cleared and reset to neutral means cutting the deck into three parts, shuffling each one individually, and then recombining them for one final shuffle.

Pick a Spread

In Tarot readings, a spread is a structure you use when searching for the answers to whatever you wish to learn. Each of the positions where you lay the cards reflects a particular aspect of your queries. There are relatively simple spreads that will utilize fewer cards, making them easy for beginners to pick up. However, the amount of detail and depth in a reading is dependent on how many cards are in your spread. The more cards you use, the more comprehensive your answers will be, but this also requires more practice and focus on accomplishing.

Performing a Three Card Spread

If you're just starting out reading Tarot cards, it's best to begin slowly. For your first attempt, try doing what is known as a Three Card Spread. Its structure is easy enough to understand since it only uses three cards. The two most common configurations involve them representing either the past, present, and future or the self, path, and potential. Consider what question you want to be answered and focus on it. Think about the intricacies of what you're asking, and speak it out loud if it helps you to visualize it. Once you have made your intentions known, all you need to do is set your shuffled deck face-down on a surface and draw a card from the top. Going from left to right, place three cards in a horizontal row.

With the first configuration, the leftmost card is the past, the middle card is the present, and the rightmost card is the future. Using the second configuration, the left will be the self, the middle will be the path, and the right will be the potential. After you have placed all three cards, ruminate on what they mean using your first impression and intuition. You will still look up their proper meanings later, but it's good to check your gut reaction. Sometimes, your unconscious mind will pick up on something you haven't realized. Think about how each card makes you feel based on their names, numbers, and artwork. Just remember that everything is not what it seems – a meaning that may seem obvious on the surface can represent something very different once you analyze it with the proper information.

Following your first impressions, refer to the lists in previous chapters to find what your cards really represent. Remember the significance of each card's placement since their traits and characteristics will inform how they're interpreted based on whether the card is revealing something about the past, present, or future. Alternatively, reflect on how the meaning can be altered depending on whether they connect to the self, path, or potential. Since you're only using a Three Card Spread, you won't have to make sense of too much information. Still, interpreting the meaning of your cards can take a few times to figure out, so be ready to try a second or third attempt before you become more comfortable with performing a reading.

Examples of a Three Card Spread Reading

In a Three Card Spread using the first configuration, if you get the Fool in the Past, the Two of Cups in the Present, and the Moon in the Future, when asking the question, "Should I ask my partner to marry me?":

- **Past:** You were open to new possible relationships and didn't stick to conventional titles or gender roles. You learned through trial and error in past relationships what you want in a spouse and what it takes to keep it healthy. You entered relationships with trust and enthusiasm but had unrealistic expectations. There wasn't much planning for the future, and the course your relationships took may have appeared foolish to others. However, even after being hurt in the past, you refused to let that hold you back and were willing to open your heart to someone new.

- **Present:** Opposites attract, and there may just be plenty of magnetism in your current relationship. You have done the dance of courtship, entwined your energies together, and felt the sparks between you both. The emotional bonds forged occurred naturally, and both of you seem to complement each other in behavior and temperament while also sharing plenty of interests in which you are of one mind. Your relationship has great affection, and as kindred spirits, an engagement or marriage is on the horizon.

- **Future:** You are creative, intuitive, and empathetic. Things in your relationship might become intense, but you need to control your emotions. There is a risk of allowing your imagination to run wild, making you paranoid and hysterical when something triggers memories of failed relationships in the past. You or your partner will suffer from extreme mood swings and become almost as unfamiliar as total strangers. Find a way to conquer your fear and temper your imagination. Use the light of reason to lead you away from the shadows of deception and despair.

In a Three Card Spread using the second configuration, if you get the Hermit in Self, the Nine of Pentacles in Situation, and the Nine of Cups in Challenges, when asking the question, "Will I get a job as an actor?":

- **The Self:** Think deeply about why you wish to become an actor. What facet of the profession are you most drawn toward? You might love telling stories through a visual medium, using your body language, facial expressions, and manner of speech to convey meaning to the audience. Maybe you wish to be rich and famous, so you view acting as a way to get there. However, being an actor can be a lonely existence. You may connect on a deep level with those who watch you, but a screen or stage separates you from them. Adoring fans will seek you out, but they cannot relate to you or to your reality. Other actors face the same issues, but it isn't always easy to forge lasting bonds when the people you work with are constantly changing. Consider whether this is something you can handle and if the result is worth the sacrifice.

- **The Path:** Reaching the level of fame you seek as an actor comes with a price. Early on, you may struggle, lacking a stable paycheck. Until you can become financially independent, you will have to rely on taking other jobs with flexible schedules to accommodate the audition process, or you will need someone else to subsidize your financial responsibilities. Once you reach your goal, you will find money in abundance and have every luxury available. Becoming self-sufficient will create a sense of satisfaction, especially if you lack financial independence before achieving your dream.

- **The Potential:** Becoming an actor will satisfy you. There will be great contentment in getting to do what you love as a career. You will have plenty of gratitude for all those who helped you succeed, and you will want to do whatever you can to repay their kindness. However, avoid the pitfalls of professional and financial prosperity. It's all too easy to let an enjoyment of luxury transform into greed and materialism. Overindulging in anything that brings you happiness can cause it to suddenly taste sour. Finding inner peace will help center you and prevent you from falling too far off the path. Remember this, and you will always know how to find your way back again.

The Kabbalistic Tree of Life Tarot Spread

The Kabbalistic Tree of Life Tarot Spread involves structuring the cards in the same positions as the sephirot on the Tree of Life. Starting at the top in the Keter position, you will lay the cards out, moving from right to left. It will look something like this:

- First card at the top in the middle, standing in for Keter
- Second card down and to the right from the first, standing in for Chochmah
- Third card on the opposite side of the Tree from the second, standing in for Binah
- Fourth card beneath the second card, standing in for Chesed
- Fifth card beneath the third card, standing in for Geburah
- Sixth card down and to the left of the fourth card or down and to the right of the fifth card, standing in for Tiferet
- Seventh card beneath the fourth card, standing in for Netsach
- Eighth card beneath the fifth card, standing in for Hod
- Ninth card beneath the sixth card, standing in for Yesod
- Tenth card beneath the ninth card, standing in for Malkuth

Each position in the Tree of Life Spread is associated with a particular trait. These connect to ten of the twelve astrological houses, with two being combined with similar houses to fit the ten-card structure. The list of which houses belong to which card includes:

- **First Card:** Self
- **Second Card:** Social Status
- **Third Card:** Unconscious
- **Fourth Card:** Home and Family
- **Fifth Card:** Partnerships and Friendships

- **Sixth Card:** Possessions
- **Seventh Card:** Communication
- **Eighth Card:** Philosophy
- **Ninth Card:** Health and Pleasure
- **Tenth Card:** Transformation

Examples of a Tree of Life Spread Reading

Example #1

Here is an example of reading for a Tree of Life Spread when asking the question, "Should I hire my nephew for a job opening at my company, even though he's not the most qualified candidate?":

- **First Card:** Page of Swords
- **Second Card:** King of Swords
- **Third Card:** Knight of Cups
- **Fourth Card:** Three of Wands
- **Fifth Card:** Nine of Swords
- **Sixth Card:** Ace of Pentacles
- **Seventh Card:** Seven of Wands
- **Eighth Card:** Three of Swords
- **Ninth Card:** King of Cups
- **Tenth Card:** The Wheel of Fortune

First Card: You need to be decisive with your choice. This is a time of positive change in your life. Don't weigh yourself down by making a decision that will come back to haunt you.

Second Card: You need to make your decision without prejudice. Do not be swayed by favoritism or nepotism. Hiring someone based on external pressure or outside influences is not a good idea.

Third Card: It's time for creativity and passion for meeting action. The person you hire should be equally as eager to do this job. While you may feel a sense of benevolence by helping your nephew, you may find yourself wishing you had gone with a better candidate if he cannot perform up to your expectations.

Fourth Card: Plans for the open position at work are already moving forward. Whoever is hired needs to be able to hit the ground running.

There will be plenty of opportunities for the new employee to prove himself, but it will only be successful if you insert the correct piece into the plans.

Fifth Card: You are going to experience a lot of stress from your decision. No matter what you do, somebody is going to miss out on a great opportunity. If you hire your nephew, your family will be happy, but you're also putting your professional reputation on the line. Should he fail to meet expectations, the anger and frustration will fall on you. However, if you hire somebody else, your nephew and your family are going to be furious with you. There will be serious tension during any get-togethers, and it will be seen as you betraying them.

Sixth Card: There will be a new and unexpected opportunity for you in this process. Success in hiring the right candidate will lead to a clear path for these opportunities. However, you must first take the proper steps to achieve it. This opportunity may not be immediately obvious, but you should trust that the hidden path will reveal itself when the time comes.

Seventh Card: You will have to take on an aggressive posture to stand up to injustice. There might be plenty of pressure on you to hire your nephew, but you know it would be wrong when there are better candidates out there. Be firm in your decision, no matter what trouble comes your way.

Eighth Card: There is going to be a great deal of sadness and heartbreak in the near future. Differences between you and your family will not easily be reconciled. They will feel bad if you don't hire your nephew, and this dispute will become a painful separation. Contemplate this loss and consider what mistakes could have been made, such as introducing the job opening to your nephew in the first place.

Ninth Card: You are a mentor, teacher, and father figure. There is great maturity and personal strength within you, which draws people to you. One of the things they gravitate toward is your ability to lead by example. Show others that you will make the right decision, even when it isn't easy. Although your paternal relationship with your nephew may be threatened, you will likely find yourself taking up this role with the candidate you hire.

Tenth Card: Fate has a tendency to spin off in new directions. New opportunities will present themselves, and there will be something unexpected in the near future. Be open to the new doors fate unlocks for you. Get ready to seize the day.

Example #2

Here is an example of reading for a Tree of Life Spread when asking the question, "Why is it so hard for me to make friends?":

- **First Card:** Temperance
- **Second Card:** Seven of Wands
- **Third Card:** Six of Swords
- **Fourth Card:** Strength
- **Fifth Card:** Nine of Swords
- **Sixth Card:** Six of Cups
- **Seventh Card:** Queen of Cups
- **Eighth Card:** Four of Wands
- **Ninth Card:** Three of Swords
- **Tenth Card:** Three of Cups

First Card: Moderation is important in all aspects of your life, including the physical, spiritual, intellectual, and emotional facets. Try to walk a middle road, finding a balance between everything. Don't be too overly eager to befriend someone. People can sense when you're trying too hard, and it puts them off. Finding commonalities with others can help you make connections, but don't pursue friendships where it only satisfies one aspect of your life. When you connect with someone in all areas, the bonds forged will remain stronger since you have more in common than if you only had an intellectual connection or a spiritual one.

Second Card: You are someone who stands up to injustice and refuses to back down, no matter how many people tell you to give up. This can sometimes alienate people, but anyone who is willing to accept unfair treatment or attitudes is not the type of person you want as a friend. Don't forget that it doesn't matter how many friends you have; what matters is the quality of the few friends in your life.

Third Card: Like many people, you carry a fair amount of emotional baggage. You might have been betrayed or lied to by friends in the past, and this has prevented you from making genuine connections with the people you meet. There is a place for bad memories and regret, but you need to transform into someone who has hope for what lies ahead.

Instead of thinking about how many friends you've lost, look forward to the ones you will make in the future.

Fourth Card: You are someone with a great amount of power. This doesn't necessarily mean you wield power but that you possess a lot of inner strength. You have a strong personal character, and you don't waver on upholding your values. Try to channel this strength and determination into working on your social life. Rejection can be scary, but it's okay that not everyone will like you. There is somebody out there who will connect with you on a deeper level because of your inner fortitude. Remember: lots of people like to eat candy, but not everyone likes to eat candy. That doesn't mean there's anything wrong with candy – you just might need to sift through those who don't to find one that does.

Fifth Card: Your lack of a social life causes you a great deal of stress and anxiety. This has become a self-fulfilling prophecy for you. You are nervous and anxious about meeting new people, so when you meet new people, you act nervous and anxious. This turns them off to the idea of befriending you, which further isolates you and adds to your stress and anxiety. It has snowballed out of control, but once you have recognized that the fear is self-generated, you can take steps to break free from its control.

Sixth Card: Surround yourself with positivity and think positive thoughts. This will put out positive energy, to which people are bound to respond. Friendships can bring both parties much happiness, and the more you share good times with them, the more positive memories you will make. This will reinforce your friendships and help you stay friends for a long time.

Seventh Card: You are someone who is calm, supportive, and trustworthy. These are great traits to have in a friend. If you continue to support others and prove you are someone they can rely on, the strength of your friendship will only increase. Compassion can go a long way to make someone interested in befriending you. There are plenty of people out there who possess the same kinds of traits, and they may just be in need of a good friend, too.

Eighth Card: There will soon be a homecoming of an old circle of your friends. This is a chance to reconnect with those people you lost touch with or reignite a friendship that has been neglected. You can find comfort in familiar faces, and that leads to more happiness. It's also possible that in reconnecting with an old friend, you will find a new one among their own current social circle.

Ninth Card: Sometimes, people grow apart. As the differences in your goals and values become more pronounced, you may simply be too incompatible anymore. It's okay to mourn the loss of a friendship, but don't spend an excessive amount of time pining for the past. There are new people to meet and adventures to be had, and there's no need for bitterness over the end of an old friendship.

Tenth Card: Good friendships include open and honest communication between both parties. Don't hesitate to tell someone about your goals, fears, hopes, and dreams. You should celebrate your friendships, both past and present, because they helped shape you into the person you are today. Even friendships that turned sour contributed to the wonderful human being you have become, so be thankful for them as well. Feel free to express yourself, and there will be someone who relates to your thoughts and ideas. This plants the seed for a friendship to blossom in the future.

Conclusion

The benefits of Kabbalah and Astrology on the spiritual development of your soul cannot be overstated. There is a reason why they've withstood the test of time. What you can learn about yourself is immense, and those who have practiced Kabbalah and Astrology can attest to its applicability in real life. The steady march of science and technology is a wonderful thing, but there will always be room for religion, esotericism, and mysticism in this world. Too much remains unexplained and undiscovered to claim they have no place in modern society.

It's a sad truth that not everybody will respect your beliefs, but that doesn't mean you should give them up. There are more than enough people who share your enthusiasm for things like Kabbalah and Astrology to foster a healthy-sized community. Be proud of the person you are and the convictions you hold. What you've learned throughout this book should only reinforce those beliefs, as you've seen just how far-reaching Kabbalah and Astrology really are. They have such a rich history that it would be folly to presume every single person across thousands of years who has practiced these disciplines was wasting their time and energy on something that didn't yield results.

All the connections between Kabbalah, Astrology, and Tarot prove that there is something more to them than meets the eye. The way things like the Hebrew alphabet, the sephirot, the Tree of Life, the signs of the zodiac, the astrological planets, and both the Major and Minor Arcana of a Tarot card deck seem to intermingle is akin to symbiotic life forms in a natural ecosystem. They feed off one another and enhance the meaning behind each of them, generating a perpetual cycle of life, just as God is described as "the beginning and the end" while creating everything in between, the interactions and associations within each aspect of Kabbalah, Astrology, and Tarot are constantly finding new minds to make new connections.

There isn't a downside to learning more about Kabbalah and Astrology. It doesn't matter whether you only have a passing interest in it or if you intend to completely immerse yourself in your studies, absorbing as much about them as possible. You can take the information provided to you and use it as a stepping stone to greater knowledge and understanding. By diving into the mysteries of the universe, you can reveal the secrets about yourself that you weren't even aware were hiding deep down inside you. Let this book continue to guide you along your journey into Kabbalah and Astrology.

Here's another book by Mari Silva that you might like

Your Free Gift
(only available for a limited time)

Thanks for getting this book! If you want to learn more about various spirituality topics, then join Mari Silva's community and get a free guided meditation MP3 for awakening your third eye. This guided meditation mp3 is designed to open and strengthen ones third eye so you can experience a higher state of consciousness. Simply visit the link below the image to get started.

https://spiritualityspot.com/meditation

References

A kabbalistic view of the chakras. (2010, April 15). Welcome to the Kabbalah Society. https://www.kabbalahsociety.org/wp/articles/a-kabbalistic-view-of-the-chakras/

ABC News. (2006, January 6). What's behind Hollywood's fascination with kabbalah? ABC News. https://abcnews.go.com/2020/story?id=855125&page=1

Achad, F. (2005). The macrocosm and the microcosm and how by means of the tree of life, we may learn to unite them. Kessinger Publishing.

Archangels - Michael-Gabriel-Raphael - fallen angels - Lucifer-mammo-asmodeus. (2016, November 7). Greeker than the Greeks; greekerthanthegreeks. https://greekerthanthegreeks.com/2016/11/good-versus-evil-eternal-conflict.html

Astrologie proved to be the old doctrine of demons, professed by the worshippers of Saturne, Jupiter, Mars, sunne and moon in which is proved that the planetary and fixed starres are the powers of the ayre, which by Gods permission are directed by Satan ... / written by an unworthy witnesse of the truth of God, John Brayne. (n.d.). Umich.edu. https://quod.lib.umich.edu/e/eebo/A29273.0001.001/1:3?rgn=div1;view=fulltext

Astrology and kabalah. (2015, September 23). Kabbalistic Feminist Astrology. https://kabalicastrology.com/astrology-and-kabalah/

Astrology and Tarot Correspondences: The Minor Arcana pip cards. (2020, July 20). Labyrinthos. https://labyrinthos.co/blogs/learn-Tarot-with-labyrinthos-academy/astrology-and-Tarot-correspondences-the-minor-arcana-pip-cards

Bakula, J. (2017, July 22). Astrology, reincarnation, and the Moon's nodes. Exemplore. https://exemplore.com/astrology/Astrology-and-The-Meaning-of-Moon-Nodes

Belloso, E. (2022, January 27). Mayan astrology 101. Luz Media. https://luzmedia.co/mayan-astrology

Bikos, K. (n.d.). The Jewish or Hebrew leap year. Timeanddate.com. https://www.timeanddate.com/date/jewish-leap-year.html

Celebrity kabbalah: No strings attached, except to the wrist. (2004, July 25). Washington Post (Washington, D.C.: 1974). https://www.washingtonpost.com/archive/lifestyle/2004/07/25/celebrity-kabbalah-no-strings-attached-except-to-the-wrist/18a6a6fc-4a87-4f18-9df8-80478f41b734/

Centre For Psychological Astrology. (n.d.). The centre for psychological astrology - incarnation. Cpalondon.com. https://www.cpalondon.com/incarnation.html

Chatterjee, D. (2020, December 17). THESE are the most masculine and feminine zodiac signs in astrology. PinkVilla. https://www.pinkvilla.com/lifestyle/people/these-are-most-masculine-and-feminine-zodiac-signs-astrology-584543

Concerning the macrocosm and the microcosm and how by means of the tree of life we may learn to unite them, thus accomplishing the great work. (n.d.). Hermetic.com. https://hermetic.com/achad/qbl/qbl-chapter-6

Fernandez, M. (2018, October 1). Reincarnation in astrology charts. Evolutionary Astrology with Maurice Fernandez; Maurice Fernandez. https://mauricefernandez.com/reincarnation-astrology-charts/

Find the sign of your North Node in Astrology: Tables. (2015, April 19). Cafeastrology.com; Cafe Astrology .com. https://cafeastrology.com/northnodetables.html

Fool Tarot meaning, love, feelings, upright & reversed – guide. (2021, March 16). MyPandit. https://www.mypandit.com/Tarot/major-arcana/the-fool

Gemstone for planet Uranus. (2020, July 23). Crystal Meanings & Healing Properties | How to Use Crystals. https://meanings.soulcharmsnyc.com/gemstone-for-planet-uranus/

Gemstones and the 4 Elements - Which one will Work for You? (n.d.). Gemselect.com.

Gemstones and the 5 elements. (n.d.). Gemselect.com

Ginsburg, C. D. (2015). The kabbalah: Its doctrines, development, and literature. Routledge.

Gnostic Tarot kabbalah. (n.d.). GNOSTIC TAROT KABBALAH.

Introduction to calendars. (n.d.). Navy.Mil. https://aa.usno.navy.mil/faq/calendars

Irving, W. (2014). The Alhambra: Extended annotated edition. Jazzybee Verlag.

Kabbalah is an interpretation key, "soul" of the Torah (Hebrew Bible), or the religious mystical system of Judaism claiming an insight into divine nature. (n.d.). New-territories.com. http://www.new-territories.com/blog/india1/wp-content/uploads/2012/05/kabbalah-sacred-geometry.pdf

Kabbalah, L. (2018, February 17). Nisan – Aries. Live Kabbalah. https://livekabbalah.org/nisan-aries/

Kelly, A. (2018a, February 2). 12 zodiac signs: Dates and personality traits of each star sign. Allure. https://www.allure.com/story/zodiac-sign-personality-traits-dates

Kelly, A. (2018b, October 6). What Houses in your birth chart mean and how to find them. Allure. https://www.allure.com/story/12-astrology-houses-meaning

Kerstein, B. (2018). Kabbalah. World History Encyclopedia. https://www.worldhistory.org/Kabbalah/

Lehrich, C. I. (2003). The language of demons and angels: Cornelius Agrippa's occult philosophy. Brill.

Levi, E. (2019). Dogma and ritual of high magic. Book I. Blurb.

Liselle, R. (n.d.). Which tree is associated with your zodiac sign? | astrology answers. https://www.astrologyanswers.com/article/arbor-astrology-which-tree-is-associated-with-your-zodiac-sign/

Major Arcana Tarot. (2021, April 3). MyPandit. https://www.mypandit.com/Tarot/major-arcana/

Mazurek, D. (2022, November 16). What do the 12 houses mean in astrology? Dictionary.com. https://www.dictionary.com/e/what-do-the-houses-mean-in-astrology/

Media, H. (n.d.). Numerology: Kabbalistic meanings of the number 9. Voxxthepsychic.com. https://voxxthepsychic.com/kabb-numerologynbr9.html

Meijers, L. D., & Tennekes, J. (1982). Spirit and matter in the cosmology of chassidic Judaism. In P. E. de Josselin de Jong & E. Schwimmer (Eds.), Symbolic Anthropology in the Netherlands (Vol. 95, pp. 200–221). Brill.

Planetary Gem Tables. (n.d.). Astrogems.com. https://www.astrogems.com/planetary_gem_table.php

Planets. (n.d.). Llewellyn.com. https://www.llewellyn.com/encyclopedia/article/76

Planets and the sefirot. (n.d.). Librarything.com. https://www.librarything.com/topic/10037

Planets ruling Sephiroth on the tree of Life. (2020, April 14). Enochian Today. https://enochiantoday.wordpress.com/2020/04/14/planets-ruling-sephiroth-on-the-tree-of-life/

Prusty, M. (2018, March 2). 9 planets and their associated gemstones for the betterment of luck. Astroguruonline.com; Manoranjan Prusty. https://astroguruonline.com/9-planets-associated-gemstones/

Sricf, R. N. I. (n.d.). Associations between the royal arch and astrology. Wsimg.com. http://nebula.wsimg.com/9df33fa1cdff047c450b000879cb238f?AccessKeyId=1892C5F96E1E5BB624CD&disposition=0&alloworigin=1

Stardust, L. (2019, December 18). Literally everything you need to know about understanding nodes in your birth chart. Cosmopolitan. https://www.cosmopolitan.com/lifestyle/a30198931/north-south-node-meaning-placement-birth-chart/

Stardust, L. (2022, May 25). Tarot cards by zodiac: See which Tarot cards align with your sun sign. Teen Vogue.

Stelter, G. (2016, October 4). Chakras: A beginner's guide to the 7 chakras. Healthline. https://www.healthline.com/health/fitness-exercise/7-chakras

Sun number in numerology. (n.d.). Astrologyk.com. https://astrologyk.com/numerology/planets/sun

Tarot cards - meaning, sun sign, planet, and element. (n.d.). Probharat.comhttps://www.probharat.com/astrology/Tarot/Tarot-card-meaning.php?card=fool

Teachers, O. (n.d.-a). Astrology. Kabbalah.com. https://www.kabbalah.com/en/articles/astrology/

Teachers, O. (n.d.-b). Meditations for the month of Aries. Kabbalah.com. https://www.kabbalah.com/en/articles/meditations-for-the-month-of-aries/

Teachers, O. (n.d.-c). The kabbalah centre. Kabbalah.com. http://www.kabbalah.com

Teachers, O. (n.d.-d). The kabbalistic calendar. Kabbalah.com. https://www.kabbalah.com/en/articles/kabbalistic-calendar/

The 1st sign of the zodiac Aries. (n.d.). Zodiac Arts. https://zodiacarts.com/elements/astrology/the-1st-sign-of-the-zodiac-aries/

The AstroTwins. (2013, October 19). The 12 houses of the zodiac, defined. Astrostyle: Astrology and Daily, Weekly, Monthly Horoscopes by The AstroTwins; Astrostyle by the AstroTwins. https://astrostyle.com/astrology/12-zodiac-houses/

The letter QOF. (n.d.). ALEFBET - THE HEBREW LETTERS ART GALLERY. https://gabrielelevy.com/pages/the-letter-qof

The letter RESH. (n.d.). ALEFBET - THE HEBREW LETTERS ART GALLERY. https://gabrielelevy.com/pages/the-letter-resh

The seven Traditional Planets. (n.d.). Archangels-and-angels.com. http://www.archangels-and-angels.com/misc/seven_traditional_planets.html

The ultimate flower astrology guide. (n.d.). Flower Actually. https://www.floweractually.com/blogs/news/the-ultimate-flower-astrology-guide

The zodiac Angels – angelarium: The Encyclopedia of Angels. (n.d.). Angelarium: The Encyclopedia of Angels. https://www.angelarium.net/zodiac

Thomas, K. (2021, November 5). A guide to the planets in astrology and what they each represent. New York Post. https://nypost.com/article/astrology-planets-meaning/

Toepel, A. (2005). Planetary demons in early Jewish literature. Journal for the Study of the Pseudepigrapha, 14(3), 231–238. https://doi.org/10.1177/0951820705053850

Yedidah. (2014, July 3). Kabbalah: A language for the revelation of the Divine light. Nehora School Audio. https://nehoraschool.com/kabbalah-a-language-for-the-revelation-of-the-divine-light/

(N.d.-b). Chabad.org. https://www.chabad.org/kabbalah/article_cdo/aid/380211/jewish/Kabbalah-and-the-Calendar.htm

(N.d.-d). Researchgate.net. https://www.researchgate.net/figure/The-Tree-of-Life-or-32-Mystical-Paths-of-Wisdom-linking-the-10-sefirot-with-the-22_fig1_236826988

(N.d.-e). Researchgate.net. https://www.researchgate.net/publication/249768878_Planetary_Demons_in_Early_Jewish_Literature

www.ingramcontent.com/pod-product-compliance
Lightning Source LLC
Chambersburg PA
CBHW072154200426
43209CB00052B/1201